MODERN CONSTRUCTION FACADES

ANDREW WATTS

Springer Wien New York

CONTENTS

MODERN CONSTRUCTION SERIES

The series is based around the Modern Construction Handbook. Themes of each chapter from the MCH are developed to provide detailed design guides for facades, roofs, materials and fittings. An additional volume of details brings together drawn technical information. Books in the series discuss component design, building assembly, craftsmanship, as well as structural and environmental issues from the MCH.

AIMS OF THIS BOOK

The Modern Facades Handbook is a textbook for students and young practitioners of architecture, as well as students of structural and environmental engineering who wish to broaden their study beyond the information provided in the Walls chapter of the Modern Construction Handbook. It shows the principles of the main facade types used today and illustrates these through typical generic details, together with a built example, that can inform a design at a more detailed stage.

The six chapters examine facades from the standpoint of the primary material used in their construction, from metal to glass, concrete, masonry, plastics and timber. Each set of three double page spreads explains a specific form of construction which is accompanied by drawn and annotated details. Throughout the book, built examples by high profile designers are used to illustrate specific principles. As is the case in the Modern Construction Handbook the techniques described can be applied internationally.

INTRODUCTORY ESSAYS

The first essay discusses some of the issues involved in working with different materials set out as chapters in this book. The physical properties of each material strongly influence the way that material is used, regardless of the façade system for which it is used. The second essay explains the relationship between manufacturers, fabricators and installers and suggests ways of working with each party. This is followed by a discussion about environmental studies in façade design and the most common issues addressed by building designers. The fourth essay on performance testing explains what is usually tested on sample façade mock-ups in a laboratory. Test mock-ups are used as a design tool as well as a check on the technical performance of a particular facade system. The final essay on double wall facades sets out the two generic types currently used, and explains how each is used. Double walls or 'twin walls' are being used increasingly to improve performance by reducing the amount of electrical energy in a building and its attendant environmental pollution.

METALS CHAPTER

The Metals chapter explores the use of sheet metal from a material fully supported on a substrate to its use as a self-supporting material in the form of profiled decking and composite panels. The use of profiled decking in thicknesses normally used for shipping containers, rather than buildings, has led to the introduction of semi-monocoque construction with this material. Some composite panel systems are being manufactured without an outer facing of metal sheet to allow a separate waterproofing layer to be added.

GLASS CHAPTER

The Glass chapter investigates the range from framed systems to point fixed glazing. Windows and shopfronts are discussed as separate systems which can be used as full glazing systems in their own right.

INTRODUCTION

CONCRETE CHAPTER

The Concrete chapter compares in-situ (cast-in-place) concrete, and its use of form-work on site, with precast concrete and its use of moulds in a factory away from the site. In the use of either technique, the constraints of the panel sizes imposing by casting methods influence the use of the material.

MASONRY CHAPTER

In the Masonry chapter the construction methodology is classified by wall construction: loadbearing, cavity wall or cladding attached to a backing wall. Within each construction method, the use of materials is very similar from brick to stone and concrete block. The differences in the specific use of a particular material are shown in the details.

PLASTICS CHAPTER

The Plastics chapter explores the range of plastic from cellular materials, such as polycarbonate, to composite materials such as GRP, which is a combination of a woven fibrous material and a polymer matrix. Newer composite materials combine the economy of plastic with the durability and stiffness of metal in sheet materials such as alucobond. The recent re-introduction of plastics into mainstream construction has been possible due to the improved quality and colour durability of these materials. An advantage of plastics in wall construction is that they can provide translucency, rather than the transparency associated with glass, combined with high levels of thermal insulation.

TIMBER CHAPTER

The Timber chapter shows both recent developments in timber walls and developments in traditional techniques. The low levels of embodied energy in this material, particularly in locally grown timber, have helped the revival in the use of this material. Traditionally shunned for large-scale applications due to its poor fire resistance, particularly in Europe, the use of timber is now better understood to reduce the spread of fire. Timber types are also discussed as their selection has considerable environmental impact.

QUALIFYING COMMENTS

The building techniques discussed and the built examples shown are designed to last for an extended period with a relatively high performance. Consequently, buildings for exhibitions and for temporary use are excluded. An exception to this principle is where a new technique has a specific use, such as cardboard structures used for disaster relief shelters. These new techniques will, no doubt, find wider applications in mainstream building construction. In addressing an international readership, references to national legislation, building regulations, codes of practice and national standards have specifically not been included. This book explains the principles of accepted building techniques currently in use. Building codes throughout the world are undergoing increased harmonisation because of increased economic and intellectual globalisation. Building components and assemblies from many different countries are often used in a single building. Since building codes are written to protect users of buildings by providing for their health and safety, good construction practice will always uphold these codes as well as assist their advancement. The components, assemblies and details shown in this book describe many of the building techniques used by the building industry today, but this book does not necessarily endorse or justify their use since techniques in building are in a continual state of change and development.

The sheet metal cladding here uses the ability of the material to form curves, rather than follow its traditional use as a material to create smooth, flat lines. This use of material looks at how metal can be used rather than how it has been used previously. The move towards non-rectilinear geometry in facade construction is set to continue, assisted by computer software that can communicate the design drawing to the manufacturing tool.

This book is intended to serve as an easily accessible guide to the detailing of facades. A few principles should be borne in mind when examining details for adaptation into a facade design. One of the most important of these is the nature of the material being used. The construction materials used in this book are described in detail in the Modern Construction Handbook, the first book in this series. The way each material is fabricated and installed into a building has led to particular material sizes and fixing methods. The value of craftsmanship and simple, straightforward solutions should not be underestimated in facade detailing, an art central to the tradition of building construction.

The two generic methods of joining materials are closed joints and open joints. Closed joints have an outer seal which is formed typically by a lap or a butt joint. This may form a single seal, as when two sheets of glass are butt jointed and sealed with a strip of silicone. The joint may also allow for small amounts of water to enter the joint and then drain down safely in a ventilated inner chamber back to the outside. In open joints, rainwater is allowed to penetrate an outer joint which is left open, but the gap allows only a small amount of water to pen-

etrate the gap. Water entering the joint is then drained away safely in a cavity to the outside. The cavity may only be a narrow strip between two panels, or may be a completely open cavity behind a series of open jointed panels. This so-called 'rainscreen principle' can be used in both closed joints and open joints, where either an outer seal or outer gap can protect joints in the cladding assembly from the worst effects of wind-blown rain.

Metals

Facade detailing in metal involves sheets, extrusions and castings used as a durable facade material. Thin sheet metal is made in narrow strips from 600mm to 1000mm (2ft to 3ft3in) wide, making it necessary to form simple, reliable joints at close centres. This is achieved by folding the metal together at the edges to form a continuous seam that projects from the wall surface and is difficult for water to penetrate. Standing seams are simple and economic to form, but need to be done with care to avoid uneven joint lines. Because it is difficult to achieve crisp lines with this method, which relies heavily on workmanship on-site rather than the use of workshop-based machines, the uneven 'oil canning' appearance can be accepted as an

uneven texture forming part of the design. Because sheet metal used in facades is thin in order to fold it and work it, it requires support from underneath. The support surface conveniently forms a base for a backing waterproof layer which is needed behind sheet metal since it is unable to exclude rainwater. Sheet metal can be welded together to form a continuous waterproof sheet material, but thermal expansion needs to be allowed for with standing seam joints that prevent the material from deforming as the metal expands.

The number of joints on a facade can be reduced by increasing the size of the metal sheet being used. Profiled metal sheet can be formed in very long lengths, and in widths up to around 1500mm (5ft). Joints between sheets are formed by lapping sheets both horizontally and vertically with sealant set between adjacent sheets to provide a waterproof joint. This allows the sheet material to span between the supports of a framed supporting structure behind, rather than needing continuous support. Fixing profiled sheet to the supporting structure requires fixings that penetrate through the outside of the sheet to the inside, which presents a potentially weak point for waterproofing. This penetration through the material by fixings is avoid-

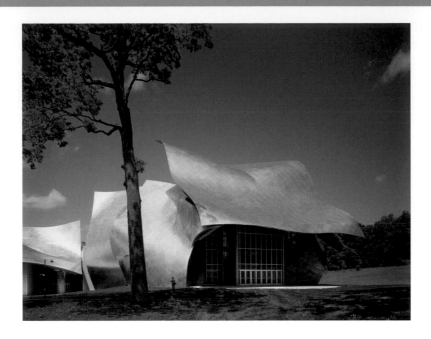

ed in standing seam sheet metal. Fixings for profiled sheet are made to be fixed easily, using a self-tapping screw, which has a waterproof washer on the outside and a drill bit on the front of the screw to make a hole. The thread bites into the supporting metal behind the sheet, while a rubber- or plastic-based washer provides a watertight seal on the outside. The self-tapping sealed screw is essential to the success of profiled metal sheeting, and corner trims and folded copings in the same material ensure the watertightness of junctions.

Sheet metal has been developed in recent years to be bonded to closed cell insulation, since both materials are used very economically in combination, so that the stiffness of insulation is combined with the watertightness and durability of metal. The successful bonding of rigid insulation to thin metal has been essential to the success of composite metal panels. These panels are joined with tongue-and-groove joints, usually on two sides. While this is a reliable joint, the joint on the opposite two sides is usually less accomplished, normally being a butt joint sealed with silicone, with an additional top hat metal profile to enhance the seal. Four sided tongue-and-groove jointed panels are more difficult to fix and more difficult to

remove if damaged. The tongue-and-groove joint incorporates a void in the centre that allows water to drain down. The basic principle with sealing joints between composite panels is to ensure that any water entering the joint will drain down an internal cavity that drains water away to the outside at the bottom of the panels.

Glass

Glass in facades is supported either by edge frames or by fixing it at points. Glass facades are beginning to be glued together without any metal fixings but the design of such structures is in its early stages, with some pioneering built examples. Frames supporting the glass must both clamp and hold the glass in place as well as prevent rainwater from penetrating the seals. Difficulties in providing reliable rubber-based seals has led to 'pressure equalised' or 'drained and ventilated' frames. Leaks in edge frames have traditionally been caused by capillary action where the air pressure inside the frame becomes higher than the outside atmospheric pressure. Capillary action results in water being drawn into the frame, causing leaks. The problem of capillary action has been overcome, not by increasing the pressure on the seal between frame and glass, but by

ventilating the void inside the frame so that any water that penetrates the outer seal is drained away safely down the cavity to the outside. The drained and ventilated cavity provides a second line of defence against rainwater penetration through the outer seal. The principle of pressure equalisation, with an inner chamber behind an outer seal, is essential to current framed glazing systems. An alternative method of glazing is to avoid a frame entirely in order to increase the effect of transparency given by the glass. Frameless glazing, or 'point fixed' glazing, fixes the glass together only at a few points, with small brackets or bolts. Glass is clamped together with a few plates, and bolted together through the joints between the glass, or else holes are drilled in the glass and the sheets are held by bolts secured directly to the glass without plates, using discs or a countersunk profile to the bolt connector. Joints are sealed with silicone in a single line of defence. While the material does not suffer problems of water being drawn through it as with clamped rubber seals, good workmanship is absolutely essential to the success of these single seals.

Walls built in glass blocks are constructed by bonding the blocks together with either a cement-based mortar or silicone.

The framed and bolt fixed glazing techniques used here create a sweeping curve generated from flat panels of glass. Curved glass is still very expensive to produce, but demand from designers will no doubt help in its development as a more economic material.

The variations in twin wall facades grow ever more complex, as with use of cast glass channels here, with an opaque screen wall behind. greater mixing of materials is set to continue in facade design.

Because blocks are set with continuous vertical and horizontal joints giving them their characteristic appearance, panels are structurally inherently weak. Panel weakness is overcome by introducing steel or aluminium reinforcing strips or rods into both vertical and horizontal joints as reinforcement, but this still limits glass block panel sizes. The principle of stack bonding limits panel sizes. This restriction is usually overcome by making the supporting structure lightweight yet rigid in order to minimise its visual effect. More heavyweight supporting structures make the blocks appear more like individual window panels set next to one another.

Windows in steel, aluminium and timber are all made in similar ways, by using a single window profile on four sides to form a frame, usually with mitred (45°) corners. Openable window lights have an inner chamber behind the outer seal which is drained and ventilated using the same method as glazed walls. When windows are set into openings in walls, it is essential to set the window into the opening in a way that avoids creating a weakness in the seal between the window and the opening. Windows increasingly have EPDM strips bonded to the edge of the window profile forming a continuous seal with the adjacent

wall surface. This method is increasingly preferred to the well-tried method of applying a single sealant material in the gap between window and the side of the wall. Windows are now expected to form part of a single waterproofing layer around a building instead of being items that are added as secondary wall components. This is due to the ever-increasing standards of construction that require lower levels of air and water penetrating through seals in windows.

Concrete

An essential principle of working in concrete is that it is a material formed in a mould, leaving a surface finish which is the mirror image of that mould, or formwork. Consequently, an important aspect of concrete detailing is to understand how formwork and moulds are fitted together. Formwork can be made to almost any shape, from plywood or GRP (glass reinforced polyester), though specially-made formwork can be expensive to make. Joints between formwork panels are visible in the finished concrete, and if this is not to be overclad with another material, then joints need to be arranged to suit the architectural concept for the facades. Complex shapes for facade panels can be made more easily in

precast concrete where, in a workshop, concrete is poured into a mould which is laid flat, making it much easier to take up complex shapes and textures which would be much harder to form vertically. Ferro-cement is capable of a high degree of surface modelling, being made as a cement mortar-based mix with a high proportion of steel reinforcement. This material is capable of providing very smooth finishes, and is more commonly used for yacht hulls.

In-situ, cast-in-place concrete is a monolithic material that provides an almost continuous waterproof surface. Rainwater penetrates only a few centimetres into the depth of the material, but in temperate climates this leads to visible surface staining. This can be overcome by colouring the concrete, adding textures, or ensuring that rainwater does not wash off surfaces where dirt can collect, which would cause staining on an area of wall beneath. Movement joints with in-situ concrete require careful attention so that they are waterproof but do not leave strong lines that are at odds with the overall concept of the facade. The facade designer must always be aware of where joints occur and how wide they will be in order to avoid disappointment during construction.

Precast concrete panels are jointed with

The greater reliability of silicone seals has led to more bold expressions of frameless folded joints as seen here.

The mixing of metal louvre panels, cast glass channels and concrete panels creates a rich mix of materials and techniques on a single facade, while remaining economic to construct.

pressure equalised drainage chambers behind vertical joints, which drain out of horizontal joints. Like in situ cast concrete, the general areas of concrete are waterproof, but the joints require careful attention to avoid their becoming too wide as a result of wanting to achieve a consistent joint width both vertically and horizontally across the facade. Horizontal joints have to accommodate deflections and movement from the supporting structure if the panels are supported from floor slabs, as is usually the case due to their self-weight Vertical joints are usually required to be thinner in order to exclude rainwater. The visual balance of joint widths, although a seemingly small issue, is critical to the visual success of precast panels. Notching and grooves are introduced around openings to ensure that windows and doors can be inserted in a way that provides weather protection as well as concealing part of the frame to avoid visible seals around the edge of the openings. Highly visible seals can also lead to very disappointing visual results.

Masonry

Loadbearing walls in brick, stone and concrete block have the advantage of being able to avoid the visible movement joints associated with non-loadbearing cladding. The absence of movement joints enhances the massive visual quality of traditionally built walls. An essential issue in loadbearing construction is to ensure that the wall is sufficiently thick to avoid rainwater penetration as well as being able to provide thermal insulation either in the wall construction or on the inner face. The sealing of windows and doors into openings follows principles of reinforced concrete discussed in the previous paragraph.

In masonry cavity walls, two masonry skins are tied together to form a single wall, and here the detailing of openings in walls is undergoing continual refinement in order to reduce thermal bridges. With the improved thermal performance of a wall there is often an attendant challenge to improve waterproofing. The top of an opening is supported with a lintel that both closes the opening and ties the two skins together while forming as small a thermal bridge as possible. Proprietary cavity closers and insulated lintels are used but these tend to match the shorter lifecycle of the windows rather than that of the supporting structure, which is usually longer. Providing a continuity between the thermal insulation in the cavity, fixed to the inner skin in the case of block-

work or masonry units, can lead to wide joints around windows, which needs careful attention to avoid visual clumsiness. This issue is easier to resolve if the thermal insulation forms part of the inner skin as is the case with inner skins in timber framing or light gauge steel frames.

In stone cladding, panels are mortared together and supported on fixings at each floor level, where each stone is individually restrained back to an inner wall that provides lateral restraint from windloads. Openings are formed by simply omitting stones and making an opening in the inner supporting wall. Windows and doors are fixed to, and supported by, the inner wall. An essential issue in detailing openings is to close the gap between the outer thin stone and the windows fixed to the inner walls. This is achieved usually by either putting a trim around the reveal in the same material as the window (usually metal) or by adding stone panels around the opening. When stone panels are used around the opening there is always a choice of either revealing the edge of the stone of the reveal trim (or the edge of the adjacent stone in the facade), or alternatively mitring the junction between the two stones. Since the thickness of stone cladding is seen only at external

The visual effect of a building facade is reversed during hours of darkness, when the building is lit from inside. Here the opaque joints between glass blocks, which reduce transparency by day, produce a delicate filigree expression at night.

corners, the choice is of revealing or concealing its actual thickness, rather than the massive stone quality the facade may aim to convey. Thin stone cladding is often used for its surface texture rather than conveying an idea of massiveness. The choice of easily commercially available stones has increased dramatically in recent years, widening the choice to thinner sandstones and limestones which have physical properties closer to those of weak granites.

Masonry rainscreens are a recent development and comprise extruded terracotta panels that are fixed in a variety of ways depending on their size. Since they are completely independent of backing walls they present enormous freedom in design. As many manufacturers have been producing rainscreen systems only during the last 5-10 years, they are still very open to development in discussion with architects and designers.

Plastics

Plastic-based cladding achieved a certain popularity in the 1960's and 1970's, presenting a fresh approach in building construction based on lightness in weight and a craft-based working method in economic materials that appealed to designers. Since then its

use has been more modest, with concerns about durability and colour fading, which have largely been overcome in the plastic-based materials available today. Sealed plastic-based cladding uses mainly polycarbonate and GRP sheet that is either fixed into frames generally used for glazed curtain walling, or is fixed together as self-supporting panels in a way similar to metal composite panels. Most types are available as proprietary systems, with manufacturers having their own details for window openings, parapets, cills and corners.

When polycarbonate sheet is used, the material often has 2-5 layers within the material that provides a high level of thermal insulation. Some manufacturers use thermally broken sections, but the more visually appealing sections have no thermal breaks. Since these sections are made from aluminium extrusions, the opportunity exists continually to improve the system in conjunction with manufacturers. An essential aspect of working with proprietary systems is that some have standard window and door sections which have an appearance that may not suit other design approaches. The challenge here is to be able to modify the windows, doors and trims to suit the overall design for the facade. Other polycarbonate

sheet systems have little provision for windows and doors and usually have no standard method of interacting with supporting structure. These have to be developed with the manufacturer to suit a particular design. Because polycarbonate is used for its qualities of transparency and translucency, the supporting framework is very visible, even with translucent wall panels, so trims to support framing should be designed as carefully as those for glazed curtain walling. In common with glazed walls, polycarbonate panels can be either fixed into frames or be fixed at points with bolts and brackets. Silicone-based sealants are commonly used to seal between panels in the manner of bolt fixed glazing.

GRP panels are also fixed into glazing systems, but can be fixed together as sealed cladding units with pre-formed standing seams like some proprietary systems for profiled metal sheet. They can also be formed into flat rainscreen panels with visible or concealed fixings. An important aspect of detailing in this material is its relatively high thermal expansion which leads to larger gaps between components than is the case with other materials. The economic nature of plastic-based cladding is beginning to be recognised in new buildings, particularly with

Standard building components, such as overhead garage doors, can be adapted to dramatic interpretation.

Construction methods, such as the cavity wall construction shown here, are increasingly being re-interpreted. The brick facade imitates forms usually associated with reinforced concrete.

the ability of plastics to be coated in different colours economically, unlike the dominant use of pre-coated coil in metal panels, but the prejudice against the material for its discoloration in older examples has yet to be overcome in architectural applications.

Timber

Timber is susceptible to more movement than the other materials described, mostly as a result of changes in moisture level within the material. Consequently timber used in facade cladding is allowed to accommodate movement as well as being ventilated to ensure that bowing, twisting and warping of timber components is minimised. In detailing timber it is difficult to form joints that perform well in tension without the need to introduce another material, usually metal. Metal pin connections, nail plates, cleats and angles are an integral part of the language of timber joints.

Although timber can be used as both cladding panels and as rainscreen panels over a different background wall, the timber boards in both cases are lifted clear of the backing wall to ensure that both sides are well ventilated. When timber boards are used to clad a platform frame, the same general principles apply as for the construction

of individual timber cladding panels, except for the vertical joints. Vertical joints between boards in the platform frame can have timber trims and fillets added that protect the endgrain of the timber from rainwater, where the timber is particularly vulnerable. Joints between timber cladding panels use a mixture of metal trims and rubber-based seals in the manner of unitised glazed walls, with a drained and ventilated chamber behind the outer timber cladding.

An important consideration in the detailing of timber is that the thermal conductivity of both softwoods and hardwoods is very low, from 0.14 - 0.21 $W/m^2 K$, compared to 45 $W/m^2 K$ for steel and 2000 $W/m^2 K$ for aluminium. Thermal breaks are not a significant issue in timber construction, which eases considerably any issues of thermal bridging around openings. This allows enormous flexibility in timber detailing with a reduced risk of condensation occurring either within the construction or on the inside face of the wall in temperate climates. Openings in timber walls are increasingly using metal trims to enhance the visual finesse of details, which can be clumsy if only softwoods are used. Metal trims can also support fly screens, awnings and related metal attachments to window and door

openings. Timber wall construction is relatively thin, at around 150mm (6in) overall, compared to 300mm (1ft) for concrete and masonry-based facades, resulting in smaller window reveals which are easy to detail with modest trims and cills. Window frames are sometimes set on the outside face of the wall to reduce any risk of rainwater penetration as well as providing internal window cills.

Timber rainscreens vary enormously from big timber sections fixed back individually to a backing wall, in the manner of an open jointed timber deck set vertically, to timber panels with louvres and sliding slatted panels. The positioning of metal fixings is critical to the visual success of all these timber cladding methods. Corner brackets and fixings have a tendency to be large in order to give a secure fixing, so attention to detail of brackets and fixings is essential to achieving an elegant appearance. Traditional techniques used lapping of timber boards, with concealed nails and screws to protect fixings from corrosion, but contemporary detailing has much less emphasis on lapping in order to give greater visual precision to the construction.

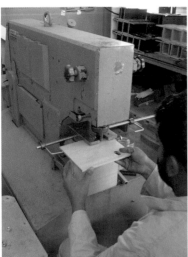

A punching machine for elongated slots commonly used in curtain wall support brackets.

A CNC cutting machine.

Where complex shaped facades are not suited to the use of scaffolding or cradles, abseiling techniques are used to seal the joints and complete the work.

er having spent considerable time and resources on a project only to be disappointed, and leaves the design team with a solution that does not conform to the approach of the successful tenderer. An even-handed approach ensures that none of the parties becomes involved in too rigid an approach.

An alternative approach for the design team is to develop a facade system, or set of systems for a project, to a detailed stage without assistance from manufacturers or fabricators. This is particularly appropriate if the building design involves a new facade technology that is an essential component of the success of the design. A team of architects and engineers can develop a facade system to tender stage with a comprehensive set of structural calculations in place to determine the section size of the most important components. The system will be designed to a stage where a set of full size visual mock-ups and a performance mock-up for testing can be constructed immediately after the tender is awarded. During the tender stage each tendering company is invited to comment on the proposed system and either accept the system or modify it until they find it compatible with their own approach. Tenderers may also propose their own facade system if it meets the performance requirements of the proposed system

and abandon the proposed solution altogether.

In some projects, the building owner or client may have a specific company, or set of companies, with whom they like to work. This approach gives greater scope for working with a single manufacturer / fabricator team that can proceed more quickly to a detailed design with visual mock-ups and results from previous performance testing on related systems.

Regardless of how the design team develops a project to the tender stage, it is essential for the design team to visit the facilities of all potential tenderers at the earliest possible opportunity. This allows the designers to understand the range of systems, skills and experience of each manufacturer / fabricator and to understand the working method of each company. These visits help the design team to understand how materials are made, worked and formed into components, and how they fit together into the final assembly. This method also helps the designers to appreciate the level of quality produced by each company.

These factory / workshop inspections are also vital immediately after tender, when the successful tenderer can again show how the facade systems or components will be made. This is very useful during the workshop drawing phase, when the design team

can work with designs from the manufacturer, fabricator and installer to give the best possible result on site. It is far easier to exert influence at this stage, in the factory, than it is on site, where changes and modifications to systems are very difficult to make. In prefabricated systems it is usually too late to push for higher quality on site, since this work has already been done in the factory. The same is true of site-based work such as in-situ concrete and sheet metal cladding, where visual mock-ups and performance testing mock-ups, as well as visual mock-ups of important junctions, should be considered at the stage immediately after tender. Site inspections for facades should focus on the correct setting out, replacement of damaged items and the fine tuning of a few interfaces that may not have been considered during the production phase in the factory. It is essential that dialogue and co-ordination occur at the appropriate time of the project, and not be left to a late stage of the project.

A tubular steel frame being fabricated to support a bolt fixed glazed wall. The smooth welding and finishing of welds, shown being done here, are essential to their visual success.

A stick curtain wall frame being erected on site. The sequence of construction is to set the fixing brackets first, then attach the mullions and transoms. The opaque panels and glazed units are fixed with temporary point fixings. Finally, the seals, pressure plates and cover caps are applied.

A bolt fixed glazed panel being lifted into place.

A twin wall facade comprising 2 skins of bolt fixed glazing supported on stainless steel cables. The support frame is fixed first, then the cables with the glass support brackets pre-fixed to them. As the glass is fixed to the brackets, the cable is slowly tensioned to the required torque.

A unitised curtain wall panel being set into position. Panels are slotted into position after being finished in the factory. Although the speed of fixing these panels on site is faster than stick framing, this method is still dependent on the speed of production in the factory.

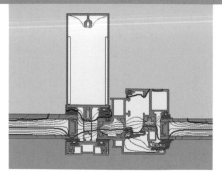 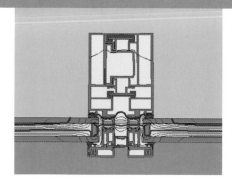 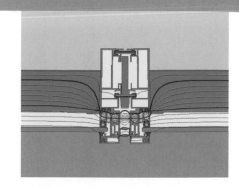

In addition to the development of design drawings for tender, together with a specification, architectural requirements and general technical requirements, the drawings and specification must be informed by both visual mock-ups and by an environmental study. In some projects the environmental study will be undertaken after tender, when a better idea of what can be afforded by the budget becomes clear. Whether the study is conducted before or after the tender process, the information required from the study remains unchanged.

Small scale environmental studies are usually undertaken as small, specific studies, usually done as a series of calculations for different conditions or different times of day or year. Bigger scale studies are structured as models, where a large amount of data is added for different times of day, times of year, or extremes of temperature, for example, to see what happens when one of the parameters is changed. The preparation of a model takes much longer to prepare than a specific 'desktop' study, and is considerably more expensive, but provides a means of interacting with the study, rather than examining a series of specific 'snapshots' taken for particular 'events' in the building facade.

Environmental studies are usually conducted on facades which deviate from systems for which performance data is readily available. As soon as one of the parameters for thermal comfort in the building is changed, the other criteria then need to be checked to see to what extent their performance has been altered. The main criteria that is checked is air temperature, humidity levels inside the building or in semi-external spaces such as atriums, ventilation levels and daylighting, including its effect on electrical lighting. If one of these is changed as a result

of a particular design requirement, such as the use of single glazing in a semi-external facade, for example, then the accompanying effect of increased internal temperature must be weighed against the benefit of natural ventilation in warmer months.

A significant part of an air temperature study is a study of the heat losses and heat gains through a facade. U-value calculations are used primarily on opaque facades, or those with a low proportion of glazing. A U-value is a measure of thermal transmittance of a facade construction, with the higher levels of thermal insulation having lower U-values. The U-value is the total insulation value of the various materials forming the construction. The formula for their calculation is as follows:

$$U = \frac{1}{\frac{1}{K_1} + \frac{1}{K_2} + etc} \quad (W/m^2 \, ^\circ C)$$

where k = the insulation value of a material measured in terms of its thermal conductivity (symbol lambda, λ) divided by the thickness of the material (L) expressed in metres.

The k value is expressed by the formula

$$K = \frac{\lambda}{L} \quad (W/m^2 \, ^\circ C)$$

In turn the thermal conductivity of a material is the amount of heat in Watts passing through a material having a surface of $1m^2$ and thickness of 1 metre under a temperature differential of 1°C. Materials which are high insulators have a low lambda value. Lambda is expressed in $W/m^2 \, ^\circ C$.

Expected U-values for opaque walls are around 0.25 $W/m^2 \, ^\circ C$, while glazed walls in sealed double glazed units, with a low emissivity (low e) coating can reach U-values as low as 2.0 $W/m^2 \, ^\circ C$, though some units are considered to reach even lower levels with

argon filling in the sealed cavity of the double glazed unit. For glazed facades, and translucent plastic cladding facades, U-values are rather less useful and solar energy passing through the facade produces significant heat gains which do not form part of the U-value calculation. The solar energy is measured as a 'g' value. Typical 'g' values of double glazed units are between around 55% and 80%, depending on the coatings and films used. Although g-values are useful for calculations, in practice architects and facade designers tend to work with a 'shading coefficient' which is often the basis for the design of mechanical ventilation systems within buildings. A shading coefficient for a facade, or area of facade, is the percentage of solar energy incident on the facade in glazed areas. The shading for a glazed facade will be provided, effectively, by the opaque spandrel zone concealing the floor construction (unless the facade is continuously glazed) and any external shading devices. Shading devices will provide different amounts of shading at different times of the day, so the overall shading coefficient is not a straightforward value to obtain, and forms part of an environmental study aimed at reducing the amount of energy needed to cool the building and air provided by mechanical ventilation. A shading coefficient of 50% is not uncommon for large glazed facades with shading devices that allow clear views out but provide some solar protection without significantly reducing daylight into the building.

The use of external shading can significantly reduce the amount of energy needed to cool buildings in summer months in either temperate climates or hot climates. External shading prevents solar energy from passing through a facade by absorbing, then radiating

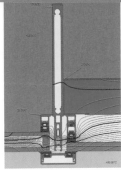
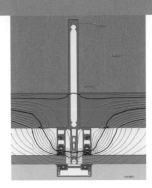
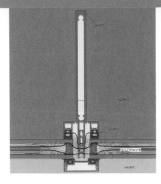

These isotherm studies for different curtain walling types show the beneficial effects of using a thermal break in glazing profiles.

and convecting solar energy outside the building envelope. In contrast, internal shading has much less effect in controlling solar gain since the solar energy has already passed through the facade and is radiated and convected back into the room having been absorbed by the internal shades. External shading is far more efficient than internal shading, but requires cleaning and maintenance, as well as being able to be removed in the event of broken glazed units being replaced. These design issues are discussed in the following section on 'twin wall' facades.

Environmental studies are often linked to the effects of natural ventilation, increased levels of natural daylighting and the use of thermal mass for night time cooling. Air temperatures within buildings are kept at between around 18° and 25°, with the surface temperature of facades being a few degrees either side of this temperature for the internal face. Isotherm diagrams are used to investigate and check variations of temperature across facade systems, and these also serve to detect and check thermal bridges across facades. Isotherm diagrams are also used in conjunction with thermal calculations or thermal models of a building, including its facade.

Humidity levels are significant in the transition from inside to outside, particularly when linked to extremes of air temperature. The relative humidity inside buildings is set in the region of between 30% and 70% depending on the internal air temperature. Dew point diagrams are used to determine where condensation will occur for the most demanding or extreme conditions experienced by the facade. This might be done in summer when, for example, it is hot and humid at 45° outside, while internal condi-

tions are air conditioned at 18°. It is essential to know where the dew point will occur to see if condensation forming at the dew point will cause any damage to the construction, and whether vapour barriers are needed in particular locations, or whether it is better to allow parts of the construction to be ventilated to either the inside or the outside. While data for established forms of construction is usually easily available, and is used by manufacturers, unusual designs or significant variations from established facade systems will need to be checked from first principles.

Levels of daylighting in buildings have increased in recent years in building types that consume a high level of energy in electrical lighting, mainly office buildings. An increase in daylighting, accompanied by a control of glare and solar energy from external shading has led to a reduction in the energy used in electrical lighting, particularly near the glazed walls. Daylighting levels are expressed as a daylight transmission factor, measured in terms of the percentage of daylight passing through the glazed facade. Daylight transmission factors of 70% to 80% are common in double glazed units. For daylighting levels in buildings and their accompanying levels of electrical light either to supplement this or provide electrical lighting during hours of darkness, the amount of light is defined for different tasks. An environmental study can investigate what daylighting levels are provided by a facade and suggest ways of modifying the design to balance daylight with heat gains and energy losses. Lighting levels are expressed in terms of lux, with office spaces having 250 lux, depending on how detailed the work needs to be, and how the lighting is distributed between general lighting from the ceiling,

and task lighting usually provided on desks, which can give up to 100 lux.

Natural ventilation is another central issue in many facade-based environmental studies, where buildings are reducing the energy consumption in heating, cooling and mechanical ventilation by increasing the provision for natural ventilation. Facade design plays a central role in this area by providing systems that can allow fresh air to enter through the facade without the accompanying wind gusts, noise and dust experienced in the built environment. The effect of heat gains during the day can be reduced by allowing the building structure and fabric to absorb heat energy mainly from solar energy, external temperature and the heat generated by building users. At night, the building fabric is cooled again by allowing the cooler night air from outside to be drawn through the building structure to cool down the building fabric. The facade is designed to allow air to pass into the building at night while remaining watertight and secure for occupants. The thermal mass of the building absorbs and releases this heat energy over a 24 hour period in order to reduce the rate at which the temperature inside the building would rise during the day. This reduces the amount of energy needed in mechanical cooling systems, and can even allow such mechanical systems to be omitted altogether in the building design. The air temperature inside the building is linked to ventilation rates, which is expressed as 'air changes per hour', which can vary from one air change / hour for small spaces with a low occupancy to 4-6 air changes / hour for public buildings and spaces where there is a high occupancy.

A test rig with additional architectural elements added to combine a performance test mock-up and visual quality mock-up as a single item.

The movement transducer shown here is set at the point of expected maximum deflection in the glazing system.

An impact resistance test on a glazed panel.

The performance testing of facade systems is undertaken for a number of reasons, the most important usually being the weather tightness of the system. Where twin wall facades and external solar shading devices form a part of the system, overall stability under wind load forms an important part of the testing. A range of tests simulate the worst conditions, and combinations of conditions, that can be expected to occur during the life of the facade. Performance testing is a check of the design approach, both visually and technically. It also assists the fabricators to understand the complexities of making the components and assemblies as well as assisting the installers by familiarising themselves with the system and allowing them to make adjustments during the construction of the mock-up at the laboratory. The test mock-up also serves as a way of agreeing how to achieve the required quality of construction, which may range from flatness of glass to smoothness of welding and surface textures. The test mock-up for a facade is both a vehicle for learning during its assembly and a checking of the required performance during its lifetime. Along with test results, which it is hoped will show the design to have been successful, there is much information that can be accumulated about ease of construction, avoiding surface damage and the visual checking of components that can inform the complete facade installation on the actual building.

The test rig

Test rigs are assembled at test laboratories that are specially equipped to deal with building facades, and so are in part a simulated building site, and in part a scientific laboratory. Facade panels are set into a test rig, comprising a well-sealed chamber, made usually from a steel frame clad in steel sheet and plywood, accessed through a door in the chamber that can be sealed. The test panel is fixed with its external face outwards and is supported by a rigid steelwork frame, usually of I-sections designed to simulate the actual fixing conditions of the facade to the primary structure. The facade panel is erected at the test facility and is enclosed and sealed into the chamber.

A measurement of static pressure is taken inside the chamber, with readings taken in a position that is not affected by the velocity of air supply into, or out of, the chamber. A fan, usually connected to ductwork, is fixed to the test rig to create positive or negative pressure in the chamber, that is, higher or lower than atmospheric pressure. The fan provides a constant airflow at fixed pressure for the duration of the tests.

A wind generator, usually a propeller-type aircraft engine, is used to create positive pressure differentials during dynamic air pressure water tightness testing. It is mounted in front of the external face of the facade panel. A positive pressure differential is where the pressure against the external face of the facade panel being tested is greater than that against the interior of the chamber.

The effect of rain is simulated by a water spray system with nozzles spaced at regular centres, both vertically and horizontally, usually around 700mm (2ft 3in) apart and set 400mm (1ft 4in) from the face of the test panel. The nozzles have a wide angle spray to cover the facade panel with water as evenly as possible.

A hydraulic jack is used to displace the test rig support beam to simulate structural movements in the supporting structural frame or backing wall.

Deflection transducers are used to measure the deflection of principal framing members to within an accuracy of around 0.25mm. Transducers are telescopic-like devices where a rod is held in a sleeve and is pushed in or out as it is held against a facade panel. Gauges are installed on a separate support frame in order not to be influenced by the application of pressure or loading to the facade panel.

Air infiltration and exfiltration

Measurements of airflow are taken at a positive pressure differential of 600 Pa (Pascals). The first test has the chamber sealed to determine the chamber leakage. Joints in the facade are taped up in order to provide a reliable seal. The test is repeated with the tape removed, but with any opening lights sealed. The difference between the two

Movement transducers set onto framing in a glazed wall in order to obtain a range of deflections across a sample panel.

A site-based hose test to check the performance of the tested system when installed in a building.

An aero engine generating strong air movement is set in front of a rack of water spray nozzles that simulate wind and rain at different pressures.

readings is the air flow through the facade. The average flow rate for fixed glazing at 600 Pa should not exceed 1.1m³ per hour per m². For opening lights the figure is 1.4m³ per hour per metre length of internally visible joint.

Static air pressure water penetration

Water is sprayed continuously at a rate of 3.4 litres/m²/minute, if internationally recognised ASTM standards are applied, onto the facade panel, with a pressure differential of 600Pa applied across the panel and maintained for 15 minutes. Throughout the test the interior face of the panel is checked for water penetration.

Dynamic air pressure water penetration

Deflection measurements are taken on several cladding members at a positive static air pressure differential of 600Pa. A wind generator is mounted adjacent to the exterior face of the facade panel. The generator output is adjusted so that the average deflections of the member matches the deflections measured at the previous 600Pa pressure differential. Water is sprayed onto the facade panel at a rate of up to 3.4 litres/m²/minute for 15 minutes, depending on the standards used. The interior face of the facade member is checked for water penetration.

In both static and dynamic tests the aim

is to check that no water has penetrated through to the inside face of the panel that could stain or damage any part of the building. Any water entering the system should be contained and be drained to the exterior. If the test is unsuccessful then remedial work is done to the design and to the test mock-up.

Impact resistance

Impact resistance is measured with a soft body impactor, which consists of a canvas bag, in a hanging spherical or conical shape filled with glass balls. The weight of the bag is usually 50kg and is suspended from a cord around 3 metres (10 ft) long. The impactor is positioned so that it hangs at rest in a position that just touches the facade panel. For horizontal or inclined facade panels, the impactor may be dropped vertically onto the facade panel. The bag is swung from the top of the rope. In either case the impact energies are the same and are usually set at 120Nm, for a drop height of 0.25m for serveability, and 350Nm for a drop of 0.71 metres (2ft 4in) used for safety. In the serveability test, for a test to be successful there must be no damage to the panel, and air and water penetration performance must not be reduced. In the safety test, no components can become detached from the system, and the impactor must not pass through the wall. The Impact resistance test is performed on joints and panels in materi-

als other than glass.

Wind resistance serviceability test

In this test, instruments are positioned to measure deflections of representative framing members. One positive or negative pressure differential of 50% of the positive or negative design wind pressure, held for 10 seconds, is applied to the panel. After a recovery time of one or two minutes, the displacement transducers are set to zero. A positive pressure differential is then applied to the panel and held for 10 seconds, in order to take the readings, at 50%, 75% and 100% of the positive or negative design wind pressure. After a recovery time of 1-5 minutes, readings are taken for any remaining deflections. In a successful test, no permanent damage will have occurred at both positive and negative applications of peak test pressure, set at the design wind pressure. In addition, the maximum deflections will not exceed the following figures, which are given for general guidance only:

General framing members: 1/175 of clear span, to a maximum of 19mm
Glazing framing members: 1/240 of span
Framing members when finished material is attached: 1/360 of clear span
Framing members for support of natural stone: 1/500 of clear span

At 1.5 times design wind pressure, for both positive and negative pressures, there

A pull-out test on a balustrade checks that the unusual design will not generate a significant deflection when installed.

An array of water spray nozzles around a glass rooflight is used to check the water tightness of silicone sealed joints.

Bolt torques of facade assemblies are checked on site to ensure that components can accommodate expected structural movement.

must be no permanent damage to framing members, panels or fixings. Glazing beads and copings will have remained in place and gaskets not displaced. Permanent deformation to wall framing members will not have exceeded 0.2% of span up to one hour after loading has been removed.

Seismic building movement test

A mid-height support beam is displaced horizontally and then back to its original position. At each stage, visual observations are made, with the test being conducted three times. Displacements, in terms of mm, are determined as 'probable' or 'credible' displacements. In the 'credible' test, there must be no permanent damage to the framing members, panels or fixings. Glazing beads and cappings must be held securely and gaskets not be displaced. In the probable test, no racking or distortion of members occurs. The panel must then pass the subsequent air and water penetration tests.

Inter-storey movement

The mid-span point of the mid-height support beam is displaced by a fixed distance vertically downwards then back to the centre, tested three times, during which no racking or distortion of the members is allowed to occur. The panel must pass the subsequent air and water penetration tests.

Wind resistance safety test

Instruments are positioned to measure

deflection of representative framing members. One positive or negative pressure differential pulse of 75% of the positive or negative design wind pressure, held for 10 seconds, is applied to prepare the panel. After a recovery time of 1-5 minutes, the displacement transducers are set to zero.

One positive or negative pressure differential pulse of 150% of the positive or negative design wind pressure is applied and held for 10 seconds. After a recovery period of 1-5 minutes, readings are taken for any remaining deflections. At both positive and negative application of peak pressure, there must be no permanent damage to framing members, panels or fixings. For a glazed wall test panel, for example, pressure plates and decorative cappings must remain securely held and gaskets must not be displaced. Permanent deformation of wall framing members must not exceed 1/500 of the span, which is measured between the fixing points, usually measured one hour after the loading has been removed. At the end of tests the facade panel is dismantled in controlled conditions to check that it complies with the design drawing. In the event of test failure, any water that has penetrated into the system is recorded.

Site hose test

In addition to laboratory tests, a facade system can be checked on site with a controlled hose pipe test. This test is conducted using a nozzle that produces a solid cone of water droplets with a spread of approxi-

mately 30°. The pressure is around 220 kPa (30-35 psi) at the nozzle with a flow rate of around 22 litres per minute. Typically, water from a hose is directed at the area of completed facade on site, perpendicular to the face of the wall. The direction of water from the hose is set 300mm (1ft) away from the wall and is directed in a linear direction across 1500mm (5ft) of the wall for 5 minutes. The test starts from the bottom of the wall upwards to determine when leaks start to occur within the system. The inside face is continuously checked for leaking. If no leaks are found, the hose moves on to the next adjacent area of facade under test. If leaks occur, the system is allowed to dry out then is completely taped up at the joints. Starting again at the bottom, the tape is gradually removed while applying water from the hose again until the location of the leak is found.

Post test conclusions

In addition to verifying the performance of the facade system, any adjustments required during the mock-up must be carried out on site. The quality of construction for the mock-up can also be used as a 'benchmark' or quality control sample for the completed facade. This can avoid many difficulties later on site, where the earlier expectations at the drawing stage can mature at the mock-up stage before installation commences, allowing all parties on the building project to agree to visual appearance and quality of assembly before proceeding to production.

The digital types shown provide a continuous set of readings during a dynamic air pressure water penetration test. The wall sample is checked visually throughout the duration of the test to check for any signs of water penetration.

Movement transducers are fixed to structural supports that are not affected significantly by the wind pressures created by an aero engine. Transducers are calibrated and checked to ensure their reliability during testing.

C

B

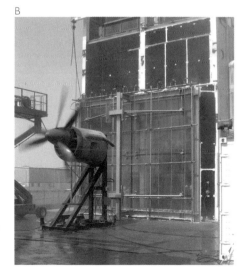

A

3 test rigs used to assess the performance of a range of wall types.

In (A) an open jointed stone cladding system examines mainly how much water will pass through the open joints, and where it will actually drain inside the cavity.
In (B) a bolt fixed glazing system has high expected deflections when compared to a framed system.
In (C) an opaque glass rainscreen wall has projecting glass fins which are being tested for their rigidity.

Isometric view of wall assembly. TYPE 2

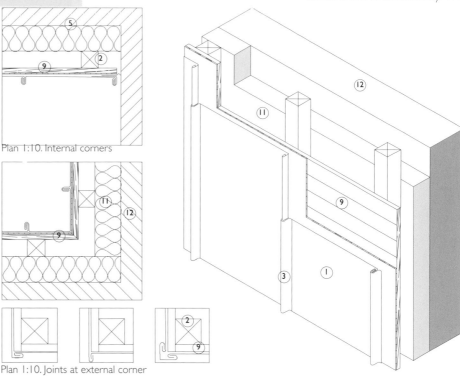

Plan 1:10. Internal corners

Plan 1:10. Joints at external corner

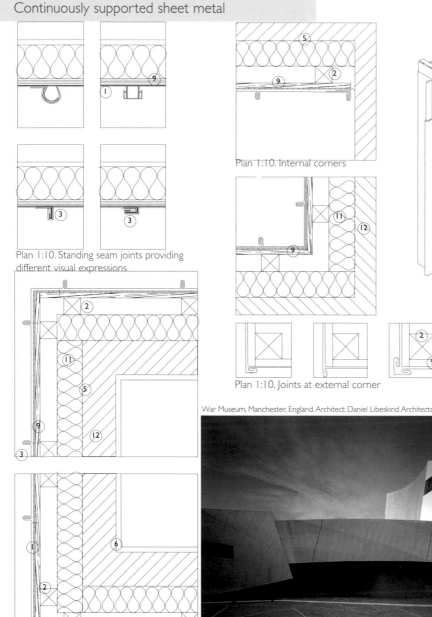

Plan 1:10. Standing seam joints providing different visual expressions

Plan 1:10. External corner

War Museum, Manchester, England. Architect: Daniel Libeskind Architects.

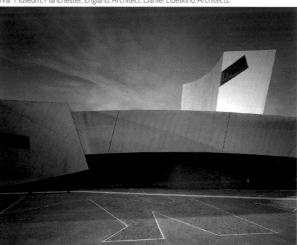

Details

1. Folded metal sheet
2. Fixing battens
3. Standing seam joints
4. Window frame
5. Waterproof membrane, typically bitumen-based paint

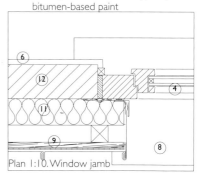

Plan 1:10. Window jamb

Sheet metal is used for the rich surface textures that can be achieved with relatively soft materials applied to a continuous supporting substrate. This method does not provide the sharp lines and flat surfaces associated with rainscreen panels or composite panel construction. The most common metals used are copper, lead, zinc. More recently, stainless steel has come into use, but primarily as a roofing material. Copper sheet is a ductile material, but not as malleable as lead. Its characteristic green patina when fully weathered gives a consistent appearance. Lead sheet is extremely durable, and its softness allows it to be formed over complex geometries and panels with a high

amount of surface relief. Zinc is durable, though more brittle than copper but is susceptible to corrosion from its underside if not ventilated. Stainless steel is a very durable material, but it still has an uneven surface when laid that provides a richness of reflection. The main disadvantage of working in stainless steel is its hardness, making it difficult to work when forming folds in jointing.

Fixing methods

There are three fixing methods for continuously supported sheet metal walls: continuous sheet, lapped tiles and recessed joints.

Continuous sheets are laid in varying widths with standing seams in vertical joints that run continuously from top to bottom of a wall. This gives the facade a characteristic striped appearance with strong shadows across the standing seam joints in sunlight. The sheet metal is fixed on the horizontal joints with flattened seams that allow rainwater to drain off easily. Horizontal joints are at distances to suit the visual appearance of the design but 12.0 metres (39ft 4in) to 17.0 metres (55ft 9in) is the maximum depending on the metal used. Vertical joints align with the edges of windows and door openings. Horizontal joints are usually staggered to form a pattern rather than try to achieve a

Isometric view of wall assembly. TYPE 2

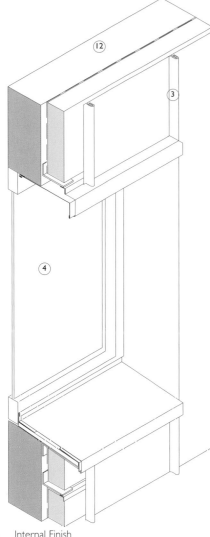

Section 1:10. Parapet and window

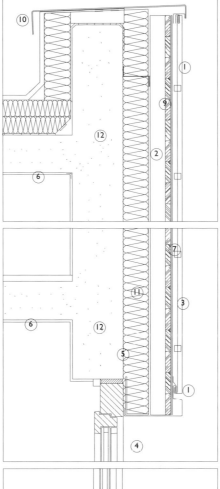

Section and part elevation 1:50

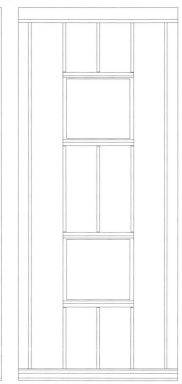

Section 1:10. Ground level cill

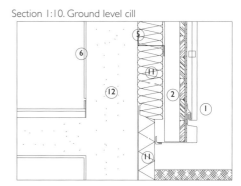

6.   Internal Finish
7.   Metal clips fixed at centres
8.   Folded metal window cill
9.   Substrate in plywood or timber board
10. Folded metal coping
11. Thermal insulation
12. Backing wall, concrete and block are shown here
13. Vapour barrier
14. Ventilated metal drip

continuous straight line which is difficult to keep completely straight and horizontal. This is because horizontal joints are broken between each vertical seam.

Lapped tiles are made approximately 450mm to 600mm (18inx24in) square and are set in either horizontal and vertical edges or at a 45° angle. Other angles can be used but are harder to co-ordinate with the edges of corners and openings. Window and door openings are usually enclosed in a metal strip around the reveal of the opening, with a shadow gap or projecting corner detail. Tiles are not folded into openings due to the complexity of jointing and the difficulty of getting them to fold neatly at half way across

the panels. Shadows across the surface of a tiled wall have small strong lines which give a very textured appearance to the facade. Tiles are lapped on four sides to give a continuous watertight joint on all edges.

Recessed joints are formed in sheet metal laid over a specially formed substrate to produce recessed lines, which are usually horizontal. The material is occasionally recessed on four sides and set on a plywood background with projecting panels formed by the plywood. However, this technique is seldom used any more due to the increased use of metal rainscreen panels with their advantage of flatness of panel and close fixing tolerances, providing crisp lines at joints

which are more difficult to achieve in a sheet metal continuously supported on a profiled background. However, this technique may find favour again due to its rich surface texture. Drips are incorporated at horizontal recessed joints to avoid staining occurring as a result of dirt being washed off the flat surfaces of these joints.

Openings

Where vertical jointed sheet metal is used, window and door openings are usually positioned so that a joint falls on the edge of an opening. This gives a clean, co-ordinated appearance to the facade, but openings that are set deliberately 'off grid' from the verti-

Isometric view of wall assembly TYPE 1

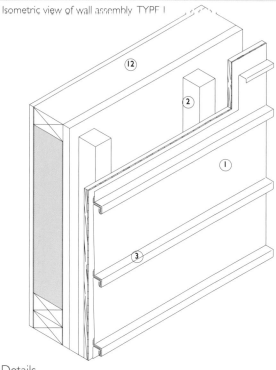

Plan 1:10. Window jamb

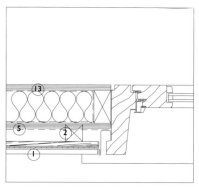

Section 1:10. Parapet

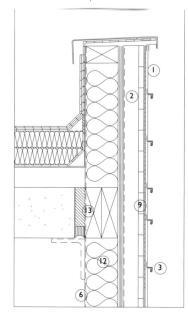

Plan 1:10. External corner with batten

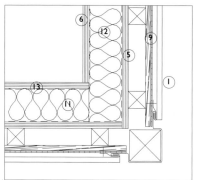

Section 1:10. Ground level cill

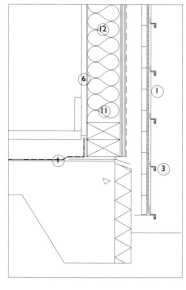

Section 1:10. Window cill

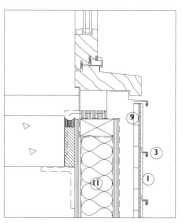

Details

1. Folded metal sheet
2. Fixing battens
3. Standing seam joints
4. Window frame
5. Waterproof membrane, typically bitumen-based paint
6. Internal finish
7. Metal clips fixed at centres
8. Timber window cill
9. Substrate in plywood or timber board
10. Folded metal coping
11. Thermal insulation
12. Backing wall, timber/metal frame with plywood facing
13. Vapour barrier
14. Ventilated metal drip

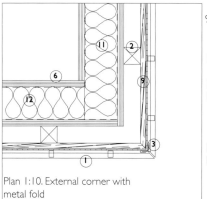

Plan 1:10. External corner with metal fold

cal joints also look visually dramatic. A recent development has been to use sheet metal with vertical joints inclined at angles up to 45° from the vertical so that they contrast with rectilinear window openings, giving the sheet metal the appearance of a continuous 'non-gridded' texture across a complete facade. For all orientations of sheet metal, window and door openings have separate metal sheets forming reveals on all sides. Although this can result in some awkward pieces of metal to form junctions around windows, in practice they are practical and economic to form on site due to the site-based nature of fixing metal sheet. Sheet metal cladding is ideally suited to the com-

plex junctions associated with non-rectilinear geometries. Attempts to make the material appear too regular can produce disappointing results, particularly where a pure rectilinear grid is attempted. In this instance, metal rainscreen panels would probably be more suitable.

Windows and doors are glazed with almost any available technique, but the ever-increasing use of double glazed units both to conserve energy and avoid condensation on the window or door surface has led to thermally broken sections being used very commonly. Window frames are often clad in the same sheet metal as used in the adjacent facade, but this is expensive since the metal

cladding will always be a decorative finish to a window that is designed for use without such a finish. The usual alternative is to use either a polyester powder coated or PVDF paint finish on aluminium to match the colour of the adjacent metal, or use a different material such as timber windows. A paint finish is obviously much easier to match if the sheet metal finish is pre-patinated (pre-weathered) so that its final colour will be very similar to the colour of the metal when installed. This is much more difficult in unweathered metals. The use of galvanised steel windows and doors with zinc is not so common due to the increased performance of paint coatings. However, galvanised finish-

Isometric view of wall assembly. TYPE I   Section 1:10. Window head   Section 1:10. Parapet

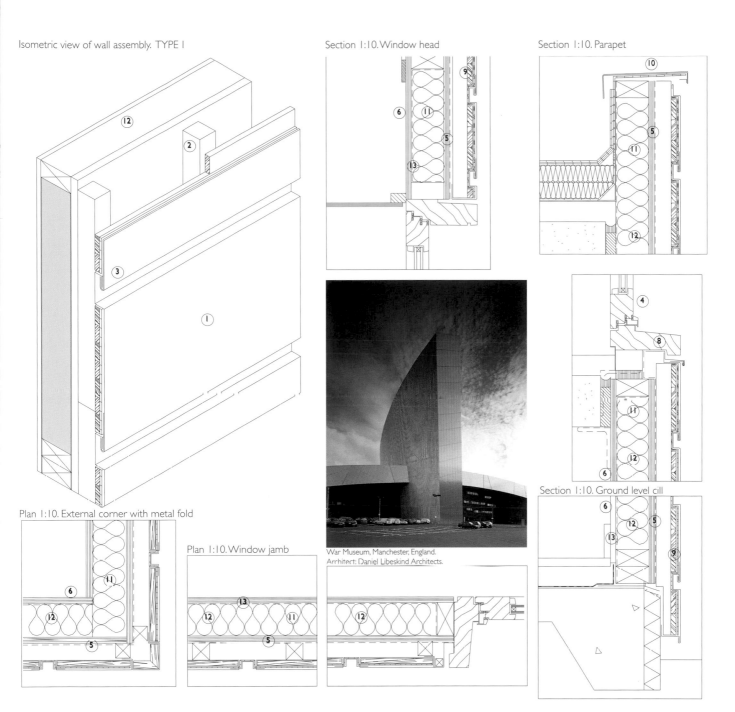

Plan 1:10. External corner with metal fold

Plan 1:10. Window jamb

War Museum, Manchester, England.
Architect: Daniel Libeskind Architects.

Section 1:10. Ground level cill

es are ever-increasing in their durability and may eventually be used as a durable finish for window frames.

Buildings clad partly in sheet metal are beginning to use large-scale glazed openings using a completely different system such as bolt fixed glazing. Where these two systems previously seemed incompatible, with sheet metal as an economic system and bolt fixed glazing as an expensive system, the two are used together increasingly where a deliberate contrast of surface texture is sought. Where bolt fixed glazing has a smooth, continuous surface uninterrupted by visible framing, sheet metal has joints in a direction at 400mm (1ft 4in) to 600mm (2ft) centres,

with a comparatively uneven surface finish.

Substrates and supporting walls

Sheet metals can be laid directly onto a substrate, typically plywood, with the exception of zinc, which needs ventilation on its interior face to avoid corrosion. Plywood is preferred for its durability, since if it becomes wet before a repair can be undertaken, the material can dry out without being damaged. Other materials such as particle boards are not resistant to moisture penetration and so are not used. Timber boards are used but are usually more expensive, as is profiled metal sheet. Where timber framing is used for the wall construction, the timber sub-

strate forms an integral part of the external wall, providing diaphragm stiffness in the frame. Profiled metal sheet is increasingly used as a substrate for zinc, since zinc is more rigid than other metals such as copper or lead. Profiled metal sheet can span the gap between the peaks of the cladding, while providing a ventilated zone behind to avoid corrosion of the zinc. The addition of a ventilation mat provides a full gap between the zinc and the profiled metal.

Sheet metal is increasingly fixed to walls constructed in a wide range of materials: timber frames, precast concrete, concrete block and lightweight steel frames made in cold formed sections.

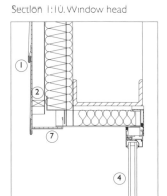

Section 1:10. Window head

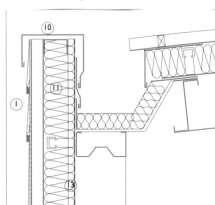

Section 1:10. Parapet

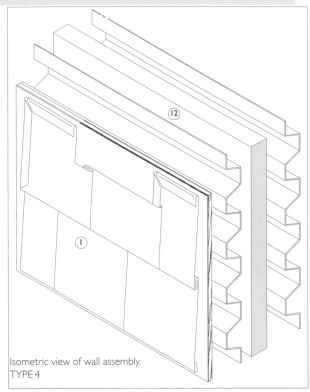

Isometric view of wall assembly.
TYPE 4

War Museum, Manchester, England. Architect: Daniel Libeskind Architects.

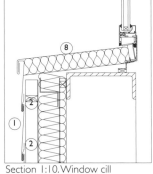

Section 1:10. Window cill

Details
1. Folded metal sheet
2. Fixing battens
3. Folded seam joints
4. Window frame
5. Additional waterproof membrane (optional)
6. Internal finish
7. Ventilated metal drip
8. Folded metal window cill
9. Ventilated layer, plastic-based
10. Folded metal coping
11. Thermal insulation
12. Backing wall, profiled metal sheet on light gauge steel frame
13. Vapour barrier
14. Steel support frame

TYPE 3
Section 1:10. Ground level cill

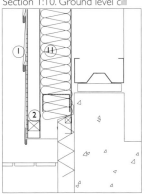

In Type 1, timber frames use sheet metal as a cladding in a fairly traditional form of construction, or as infill panels to a timber, concrete or steel frame. The overall cross section of the wall remains thin due to the inclusion of thermal insulation within the frame rather than on an outside face. A vapour barrier is needed on the warm-in-winter side (in a temperate climate) to avoid vapour reaching the insulation from inside. The vapour barrier is needed in the same place in Type 3, where pressed steel, or 'light gauge' steel sections are used. The all-metal construction of Type 3 is undergoing refinement for use in housing, where almost all its components can be either recycled or

unbolted and modified with the same kit of parts during its lifetime. Its flatness of appearance combined with small-scale standing seam joints make it ideal for a sealed metal cladding where profiled metal sheet or composite panels have too 'industrial' an appearance. In Type 2, thermal insulation is set on the outside of the concrete structure in order to use its thermal mass as well as to keep the structure at as even a temperature as possible. The metal cladding is then set forward of the insulation. A new development is the use of profiled metal cladding as a substrate in Type 4. Where zinc is used the void formed by the profiled sheet provides a ventilation zone without

the use of timber. A plastic-based drainage mat is set between the zinc and the profiled sheet to complete the ventilation.

Corners, parapets and cills
Sheet metal can be joined at corners in facades with either recessed or projecting coverstrips. The covers need a timber or plywood support under them to provide rigidity. Corners for vertically set metal sheet can also be formed by setting standing seam joints at the corner, or close to the corner on either side of the edge. With tiled sheets, corners usually wrap around, ignoring the corner like a continuous pattern folded around the corner. Alternatively, corners can

Isometric view of wall assembly. TYPE 4

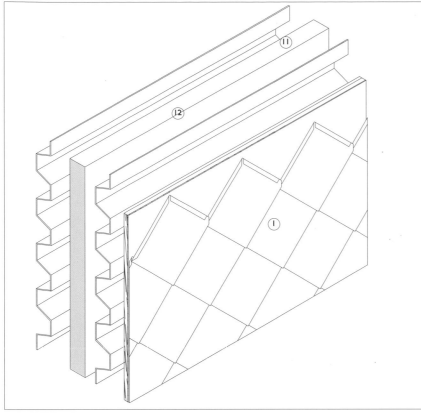

Section 1:10. Window jamb

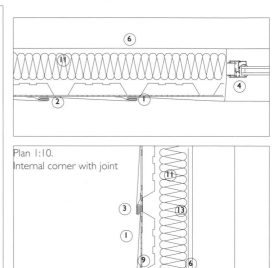

Plan 1:10.
Internal corner with joint

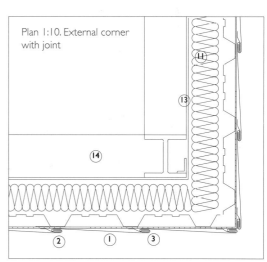

Section 1:10. Wall

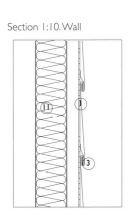

Plan 1:10. External corner
with metal fold

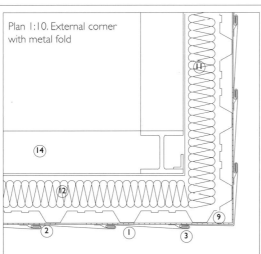

Plan 1:10. External corner
with joint

have coverstrips that break the pattern from one facade to another. There is an increased use of pressed metal clips and rails, as used in profiled metal cladding, to support sheet metal substrates, typically plywood. Clips and rails are made as proprietary systems which can be fixed to the backing wall quickly and easily adjusted to correct vertical or inclined alignment.

An advantage of sheet metal is that parapet copings and cill drips at the base of walls at windows can be formed in the same material with an identical finish. This is unlike many other metal cladding systems, where extruded aluminium or pressed steel or aluminium are most commonly used for parapets and cills. The ability to form metal on site in junctions of sheet metal walls with parapet copings is used either to form a recessed joint, which allows the standing seam joint in the cladding to be tapered down to the line of the coping, or a projecting parapet coping which allows the standing seam to butt up to the underside of the coping. With either solution, an undercloak flashing or waterproof layer is needed underneath the coping to provide additional waterproofing.

Cills are formed in a similar way, but with projecting or flush drips to throw water clear of the base of the cladding. Where unweathered metal is used, care should be taken that rainwater runoff from oxidising metal does not stain paved surfaces at the base of the wall. Slot drains or gravel edges can be used both to provide drainage and avoid visible staining. Drips are often reinforced with a steel or aluminium angle to create a strong, straight edge. Compatibility between the cladding material and support material must be ensured to avoid bimetallic corrosion. Where the void behind metal cladding is used for ventilation, parapets and cills are used to introduce fresh air. Insect mesh is introduced within the joint, but its presence does not alter air flow rates significantly.

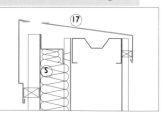

Mini-House, Nerima-ku, Tokyo, Japan. Architect: Yoshiharu Tsukamoto and Momoyo Kaijima / Atelier Bow-Wow, TIT Tsukamoto Lab.

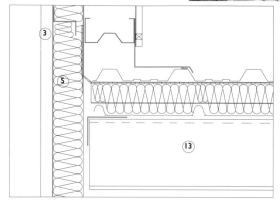

Section 1:10. Parapet and ground level cill

Profiled sheet types

Plan 1:10. External corner

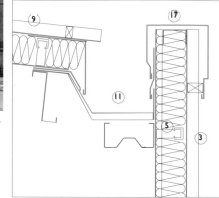

Section 1:10. Parapet and cill

Section 1:10. Roof junction at gable end

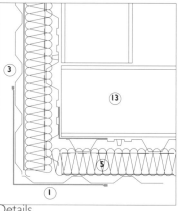

Details

1. Metal cover strip set
2. Horizontally-set profiled sheet
3. Vertically-set profiled sheet
4. Z section steel fixing rails
5. Thermal insulation
6. Backing wall, typically timber/metal frame with ply wood facing and waterproof membrane, or concrete block
7. Vapour barrier
8. Internal finish
9. Roof, typically profiled metal sheet
10. Curved eaves profile
11. Concealed gutter
12. Exposed gutter

An advantage of profiled metal cladding is that it can be easily integrated with a similar system used for cladding the roof. Also, small areas of roof can be easily accommodated as steps within the facade with simple junctions between vertical and shallow pitch roofs. At the junction with the top of the roof an undercloak flashing is used to ensure water running off the wall is sent on down the roof and not into the joint at the base. At the bottom of the roof, either an exposed gutter or a concealed parapet gutter is used to collect the rainwater. Very small areas of roof can be drained without a gutter by projecting the roof beyond the cladding, allowing the rainwater to be thrown clear of the cladding and avoiding staining of the wall below. The effect of throwing water clear of the building needs to be integrated within the overall design.

Profiled metal cladding is most commonly used in large single storey buildings such as factories or warehouses where it spans vertically from ground to roof without the need for additional support. This makes it a very economical solution for enclosing these building types. Although profiled metal cladding is used mainly for industrial buildings in conjunction with a portal frame in either steel or concrete, it provides an economic cladding system for larger framed structures.

The material can be set either vertically or horizontally to suit the design.

Horizontally-set cladding is used where its strong horizontal lines are used for linear emphasis. Like vertically-set cladding, the profiled sheet is supported at 3.0 to 5.0 metre (10ft to 16ft 6in) centres by posts or structural columns. This direction allows the material to enclose a building with a curved section. A useful aspect of profiled metal sheeting is its ability to be curved in one direction. This makes it an ideal cladding material for buildings with a curved vertical section. Slight irregularities in the surface finish or setting out of the curve is concealed by the profile itself. Polished stainless steel has been used for horizontally-set cladding in public buildings where its high cost is bal-

Section 1:10. Curved eaves with parapet

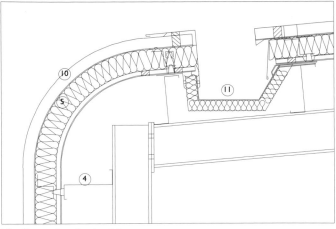

13. Supporting structural frame
14. Structural slab
15. Window frame
16. Metal trim to window
17. Metal parapet coping

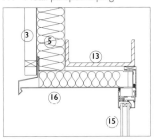

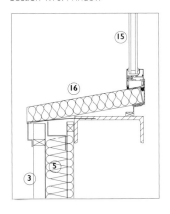

Section 1:10. Window

Isometric view of wall assembly

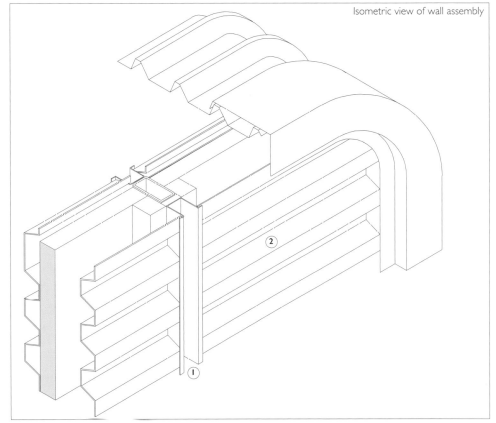

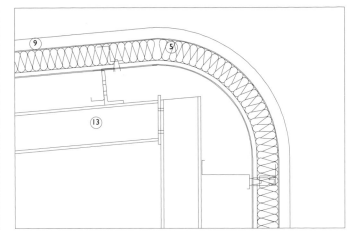

anced by longer durability than coated aluminium or coated mild steel types.

Vertically-set sheeting has horizontal cladding rails at 3.0 metre to 5.0 metre (10ft to 16ft 6in) centres, depending on the floor height. In buildings of more than one storey, an inner lining to the wall is usually added since the gap created between the cladding and the floor slab is difficult to seal economically at floor level in a way that will allow people to walk on it. The additional inner lining may extend up to 1.0 metres (3ft 3in) above finished floor level and may be either a metal lining tray forming part of the proprietary cladding system, or be a concrete blockwork wall around 100mm (4in) thick. A

smoke seal or fire barrier may be required between the floors enclosed by the cladding but this is very much dependent upon its particular application. Although horizontal rails can be set at wide centres, additional rails may be needed either to accommodate windows and doors or to increase the stiffness of the wall without using a much deeper profile, which would also increase stiffness.

Junctions

When laid vertically, sheets are joined by lapping them by around 150mm (6in) at vertical joints. Horizontal joints are also lapped with the upper sheet set over the lower one in the traditional manner. When laid horizon-

tally, horizontal joints are formed with laps as when laid vertically, but horizontal joints are not usually lapped in the same way. This is mainly because it is difficult to form a continuous straight line in a joint that moves in and out with the shape of the profile. Instead a recessed top hat section or projecting coverplate is used. The profiled sheet is butted up to the C-shaped section and sealed with silicone or mastic. The same principle is used for a projecting coverplate.

Corners are treated in a similar way. Corners to vertically- and horizontally-set cladding use projecting or recessed coverstrips. The profiled sheets that meet are lapped, however, to provide a weathertight

Section 1:10. Roof junction at gable end

Section 1:10. Roof junction at abutting wall

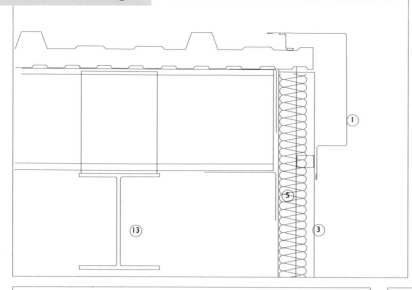

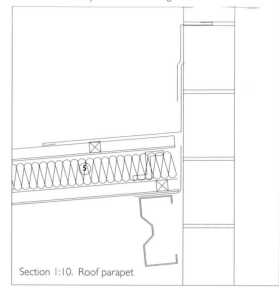

Section 1:10. Roof parapet

Section 1:10. External gutter

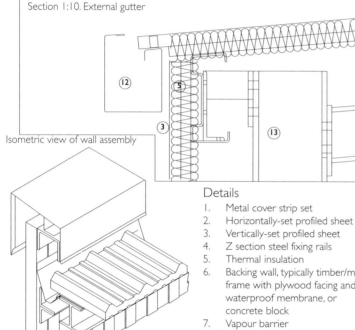

Isometric view of wall assembly

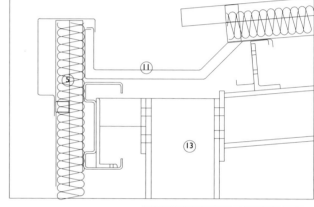

Plan 1:10. Door opening

Details

1. Metal cover strip set
2. Horizontally-set profiled sheet
3. Vertically-set profiled sheet
4. Z section steel fixing rails
5. Thermal insulation
6. Backing wall, typically timber/metal frame with plywood facing and waterproof membrane, or concrete block
7. Vapour barrier
8. Internal finish
9. Roof, typically profiled metal sheet
10. Curved eaves profile
11. Concealed gutter
12. Exposed gutter
13. Supporting structural frame
14. Structural slab
15. Window frame
16. Metal trim to window
17. Metal parapet coping

seal, and the coverplate provides both an additional seal along a potentially vulnerable joint as well as a crisp line to the corner. Regardless of sheet orientation, edging and jointing pieces are clearly visible, making them an important part of the design. Whereas profiled sheet can be lapped to give a continuous appearance on a large area of facade, the edging and jointing pieces of parapets, cills and corners are clearly visible. The visual impact of these junctions can be reduced with recessed joints. The use of curved eaves sheets and curved (in plan) corner sheets was developed to avoid the need for visible corner pieces. 90° corner sheets are now available, from some manufacturers, that can

be lapped smoothly over adjacent profiled metal sheets.

Parapets and gutters

Parapets are usually formed by projecting the profiled sheet above the roof line in order to conceal the roof completely, which is often in the same material in the case of industrial buildings. Alternatively, a low parapet is formed at the level of the intersection of wall and roof, with a recessed gutter set immediately behind the parapet. A variation on this latter solution is to use curved eaves to give the idea of complete continuity between walls and roof with only a recessed gutter creating a line between the two. The

recessed gutter in any of these configurations is useful when a pitched roof is used. On the gable elevation the parapet can remain the same height while the roof rises and falls independently of the continuing line of the parapet on all sides. Curved eaves have mitred corner panels to allow a curved profile to be used continuously around a building.

Visible gutters are fixed on the outside face of the cladding. The roof projects over the top of the cladding in order to drain rainwater into the gutter, resulting in the roof visually projecting forward of the wall, unlike a parapet gutter. An advantage of this method is that rainwater is kept outside the

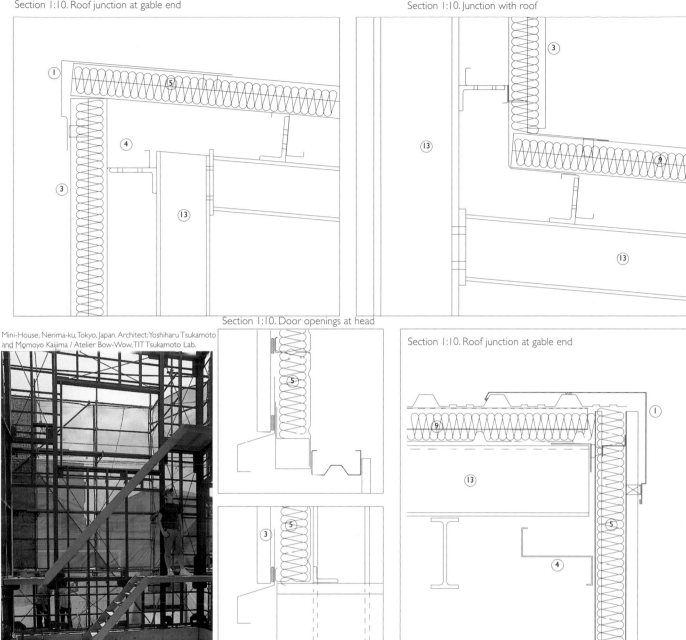

Section 1:10. Roof junction at gable end

Section 1:10. Junction with roof

Mini-House, Nerima-ku, Tokyo, Japan. Architect: Yoshiharu Tsukamoto and Momoyo Kaijima / Atelier Bow-Wow, TIT Tsukamoto Lab.

Section 1:10. Door openings at head

Section 1:10. Roof junction at gable end

building, avoiding the need to run vertical rainwater pipes within a building, then running rainwater back out through the foundations below ground level. Since gutters are needed only at the base of roof slopes, gutters are often not needed on all facades, giving an uneven appearance to the building. A solution to making gutters work on all facades is to design a hipped roof that drains equally into all gutters, but this can complicate roof design. Gutters require support by brackets back to primary structure in order to support the weight of water when in use. The supporting brackets usually need to penetrate the cladding, requiring seals around the penetrations in order to make

them weathertight. If the roof construction is required to be ventilated then the depth of the gutter will increase if the roof is intended to be hidden from view. Deep gutters have a strong visual presence on the facade.

Window and door openings

The reveals for windows and doors are formed in flat metal sheet, usually the same metal and same colour as the profiled sheeting. In practice the colour matching can be difficult if the coating (usually polyester powder coating or PVDF) is applied in different workshops or by different coating applicators. Contrasting colours are sometimes chosen for this reason. This is also true of

window sections, which are usually supplied predated by a different manufacturer. Close co-ordination is needed between contractors to ensure a consistent colour throughout the project. An alternative approach is to reduce reveals to a small depth and use a colour for the windows different from that of the adjacent cladding. For example, with a silver metallic finish for cladding, a darker grey might be used for window frames without creating any contrast between the two colours used.

Cills are formed in pressed metal which is inclined to drain water from its horizontal surface and has a projecting drip to avoid dirt, washed off the cill, running onto the

Isometric view of window

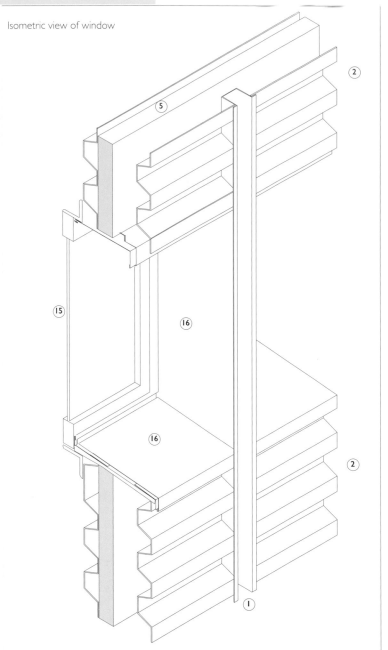

Mini-House, Nerima-ku, Tokyo, Japan.
Architect: Yoshiharu Tsukamoto and
Momoyo Kaijima / Atelier Bow-
Wow, TIT Tsukamoto Lab.

Isometric view of door openings

Details

1.   Metal cover strip set
2.   Horizontally-set profiled sheet
3.   Vertically-set profiled sheet
4.   Z section steel fixing rails
5.   Thermal insulation
6.   Backing wall, typically
     timber/metal frame with ply
     wood facing and waterproof
     membrane, or concrete block
7.   Vapour barrier
8.   Internal finish
9.   Roof, typically profiled
     metal sheet
10. Curved eaves profile
11. Concealed gutter
12. Exposed gutter
13. Supporting structural frame
14. Structural slab
15. Window frame
16. Metal trim to window
17. Metal parapet coping

cladding below, which would cause staining. Some drips have rising edges at the sides to avoid water running off at the sides that causes streaking in lines below the edges of the openings. Cills at ground level or at the base of the cladding are either flush or projecting, to suit visual requirements. As with sheet metal cladding, the cill is usually reinforced both to ensure it lies in a straight line and protect it from accidental damage.

Insulation and liner trays

Although profiled metal sheet is capable of long vertical spans, the thermal insulation and internal finish material require additional support. The insulation cannot be fixed directly

to the metal sheet without being bonded to it. Fixing brackets to the profiled sheet would involve penetrating the sheet, creating a possible point for water ingress. Welding a support bracket would be both expensive and easily distort the surface of the cladding. Bonding the insulation to the liner would be the next practical method, but this is done as a composite panel, which has constraints and is dealt with in the next section.

Flexible insulation quilt is fixed to intermediary sheeting rails that are also used to support an inner metal lining sheet. Sheeting rails are made from pressed steel sections. Since the lining sheets are usually flat, to create a smooth finish within the building, they

do not span very far and require sheeting rails set at close centres. The rails can be used to give additional rigidity to the outer profiled sheet, but this requires penetrating the sheet with screw fixings which are sealed from the outside with plastic caps and washers.

An inner lining tray can also be formed from the same metal profiled sheet, as used in warehouse buildings where a smooth inner wall finish is not needed. Some intermediary sheeting rails are still required to support the thermal insulation. A more economic form of lining wall that does not interfere with the outer profiled cladding is concrete blockwork. In this instance, closed cell

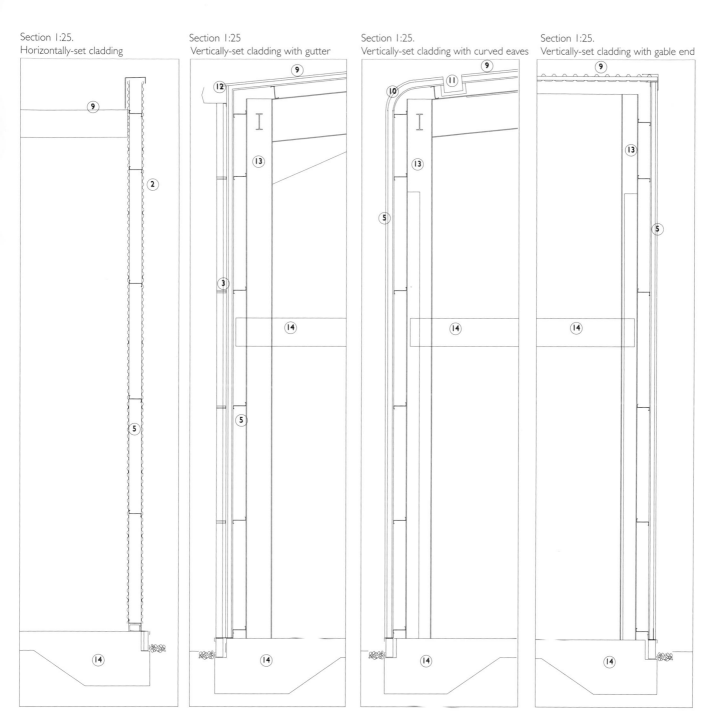

Section 1:25.
Horizontally-set cladding

Section 1:25
Vertically-set cladding with gutter

Section 1:25.
Vertically-set cladding with curved eaves

Section 1:25.
Vertically-set cladding with gable end

thermal insulation is fixed to the outside face of the wall.

Developments

The range of profile types is steadily increasing, with wider, deeper profiles that were originally designed for use as roof decking being used as wall cladding. However, some of the interlocking types used on roofs are not suited to cladding since the standing seam joint, which is not designed to be tightly folded together, does not work when set in the vertical plane. This principle is also true of wall cladding types which are lapped and are not suited to use in roofs, where the seam is not high enough to be submerged under water during rain. A recent development has been the use of flat metal rainscreen panels fixed directly to a profiled sheet. This provides a smooth finish visually to the outside face of the cladding, while maintaining the economy and structural efficiency of the profiled sheet. Although the outer metal panel is fixed to the profiled sheet with screws or rivets that penetrate it, the pin jointed rainscreen configuration protects the fixings from the worst effects of windblown rain.

Details
1. Vertically-set composite panel
2. Horizontally-set composite panel
3. Silicone-based seal
4. Outer metal facing
5. Inner metal facing
6. Inner insulation core
7. Metal capping
8. Concealed fixing
9. Supporting structure
10. 4-way interlocking composite panel
11. Window frame
12. Sectional roller shutter formed from composite panels
13. Roof construction, composite panels are shown
14. Metal trim
15. Exposed gutter
16. Concealed gutter
17. Metal parapet coping
18. Stick glazed curtain walling
19. Door frame

Isometric view of assembly: Panels spanning vertically with interlocking joints on vertical edges

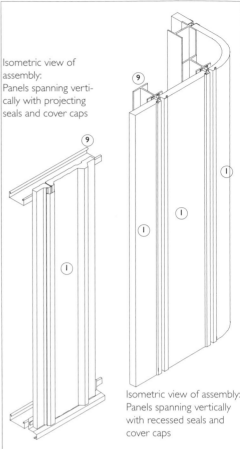

Isometric view of assembly: Panels spanning vertically with projecting seals and cover caps

Isometric view of assembly: Panels spanning vertically with recessed seals and cover caps

Telecom Authority Building, Oporto, Portugal.
Architect: João Álvaro Rocha and José Manuel Gigante.

Composite metal panels require fewer components than for the 'kit of parts' used in the assembly of profiled metal cladding. Like profiled metal, panels are set either vertically or horizontally. Some panels interlock on two sides, while others interlock on four sides. Four-sided panels require no separate interface components for jointing but it is more difficult later to remove a damaged panel.

Horizontally-set composite panels can be easily integrated with ribbon windows and suit building facades covering several floors. Panels are stacked one above the other with their vertical joints closed by rubber-based gaskets, recessed channel sections in aluminium, or projecting coverstrips in aluminium.

Panels are fixed back to primary structure or on a secondary steel frame, typically box sections, fixed to the sides of floor slabs if columns are spaced too far apart or columns are not positioned on the edge of floor slabs.

Where windows are used in a facade, additional support is needed to frame the opening. This is because windows are not supported by the composite panels except where made specifically as part of a proprietary system. In practice, windows are usually supplied by a specialist manufacturer.

The steel support framing is set on the face of the slab, making it easier to take up deflections in floor slabs. However, as is the case with curtain walling, the gap between composite panel and floor slab needs filling with a smoke seal or fire barrier. The floor finish usually has a metal angle to close off the gap at slab level and at the soffit level below. Four-sided interlocking panels use the same principle for fixing on all four sides. This also makes it easier to integrate windows within the system since a window panel is locked in like any other panel.

Vertically-set composite panels are more common in single storey applications, but multi-storey applications are used increasingly. Panels are interlocked at vertical joints, while horizontal joints are formed by using a cill-type detail similar to that used in a transi-

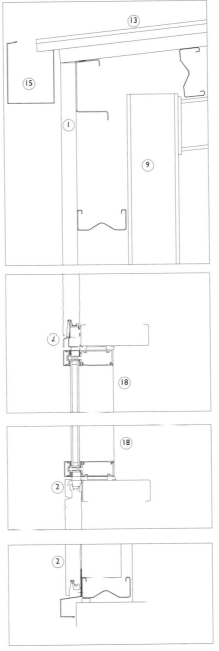

Section 1:10. Parapet and cill with curtain walling-type window set into cladding, typical in industrial applications

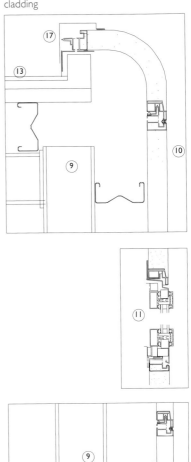

Section 1:10. Curved parapet and cill with aluminuim window set into reveal in cladding

Section 1:10. Parapet and door opening. Sectional roller shutter door shown, typical in industrial applications

tion from vertical panel to low pitched roof. A cill in extruded or folded aluminium or steel (depending on which metal is used for the composite panel faces) is used. The front of the trim projects beyond the face of the cladding to throw water clear and prevent staining to panels below. The back of the drip projects up the back of the upper panel to prevent water from penetrating the joint. Panels are also supported on either an interlocking frame or occasionally they span between columns if panels are stiff enough to span unassisted. An additional method of fixing panels is to position them between floor slabs spanning from floor to ceiling when used as part of a rainscreen system.

Panels sit on the floor slab with their outer face flush with the edge of the slab. The outer rainscreen is set forward of the composite panel, concealing both the panels and the edge of the floor slab.

Interlocking vertically-set panels are of several types, unlike horizontally-set types, which have a stepped joint to avoid rainwater penetration. The most common type for vertical joints is also a stepped joint with a recess on the outer face. An alternative is to have projecting nibs on the sides of the panel to which a coverplate is fixed over the gap between the two panels. Rubber-based seals are set into the depths of all these joint types. Another joint is a C-shaped channel profile which interlocks with the profile of the adjacent panel. The outside face of the panel has a slightly projecting edge instead of a recessed joint in the stepped joint types.

All these panel types use jointing methods that avoid thermal bridges. Drips often penetrate from outside but the low condensation risk is assessed during the design stage.

Parapets and cills

Parapet copings and drips at ground level can also be made as composite panels, forming an integrated part of a proprietary system. This can be an advantage when seeking a seamless effect across a facade, but sets

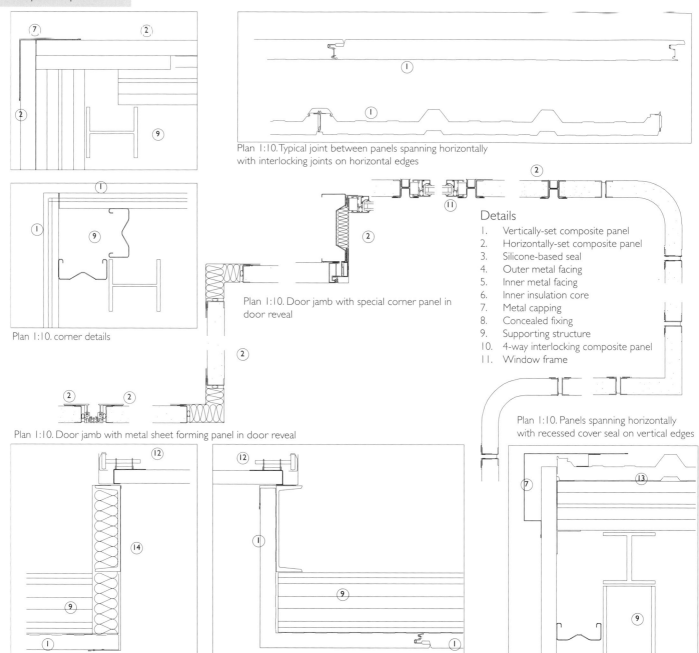

Plan 1:10. Typical joint between panels spanning horizontally with interlocking joints on horizontal edges

Plan 1:10. corner details

Plan 1:10. Door jamb with special corner panel in door reveal

Plan 1:10. Door jamb with metal sheet forming panel in door reveal

Plan 1:10. Panels spanning horizontally with recessed cover seal on vertical edges

Details
1. Vertically-set composite panel
2. Horizontally-set composite panel
3. Silicone-based seal
4. Outer metal facing
5. Inner metal facing
6. Inner insulation core
7. Metal capping
8. Concealed fixing
9. Supporting structure
10. 4-way interlocking composite panel
11. Window frame

nal face is smooth and gridded, the supporting structure is visible and usually set on the inside face to avoid penetrations to the outside through the joints between panels. If the exposed structure is enclosed with an economic lining wall concealing the structure, this additional element can add considerable cost to the cladding, making it much less economic.

For this reason, supporting structure that is designed to be seen, such as tubular steel posts, is increasingly used. The composite panels span between steel posts or trusses with little or no interlocking supporting structure. In order to keep the supporting structure as visually elegant as possible, truss-

es or posts are spaced as far apart as possible. This has led to panels getting longer, with a maximum length currently around 15 metres (49ft). Some proprietary systems include edges to panels which are deeper, making the continuous vertical joints and horizontal joints more rigid, allowing them to span greater distances, thus reducing the amount of visible supporting structure needed.

Increasingly, window openings need not be dictated by the direction in which panels are laid. Horizontally-set panels do not have windows arranged horizontally. Transitions between window openings and composite panels are becoming more economic with

standard extrusions and rubber-based seals. This is ever-more the case with four-sided, interlocking panels, where window panels and metal panels are fixed in the same way. Increasingly, irregular facade grids are being developed in designs to create a richer mix of panel sizes in visual patchwork of different sizes of panels.

Corners

Composite panels are connected at corners by one of two methods. Either specially made corner panels are used (typically why 90° is standard) or a coverstrip is added to cover the junction where the panels meet. Corner panels are more suited to vertically-

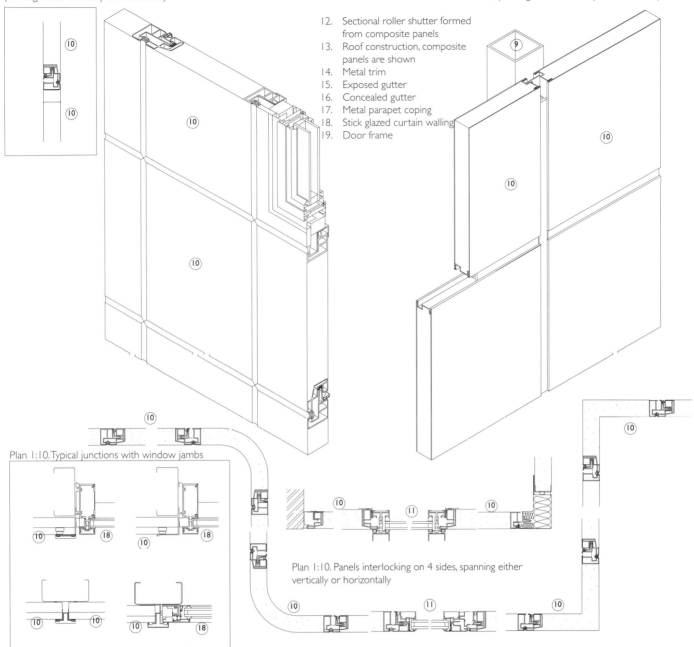

Isometric view of assembly: Panels interlocking on 4 sides, spanning either vertically or horizontally

Isometric view of assembly: Panels semi-interlocking on 4 sides, with baffle seals, spanning either vertically or horizontally

12. Sectional roller shutter formed from composite panels
13. Roof construction, composite panels are shown
14. Metal trim
15. Exposed gutter
16. Concealed gutter
17. Metal parapet coping
18. Stick glazed curtain walling
19. Door frame

Plan 1:10. Typical junctions with window jambs

Plan 1:10. Panels interlocking on 4 sides, spanning either vertically or horizontally

set arrangements, though panels for horizontally-laid panels are sometimes used for visual effect. Where corner cover strips are used, their appearance resembles that of profiled metal cladding, which can give a facade an overall framed appearance. Metal trims at the parapet, base and corners can give this appearance. For this reason, the special corner panels and parapet panels are used increasingly.

Thermal bridges at cills

A weakness in composite panels systems has been the use of pressed metal sections or aluminium extrusions that pass from outside to inside without a thermal break. This is

being remedied by the use of insulated cills, made in the manner of composite panels. This reduces the thermal bridge, in some cases a break in the section from outside to inside can be formed by turning the metal cill into the injected foam or polystyrene in the same way as a composite panel.

Telecom Authority Building, Oporto, Portugal.
Architect: João Álvaro Rocha and José Manuel Gigante.

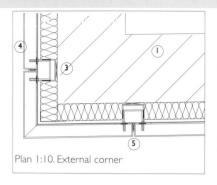

Plan 1:10. External corner

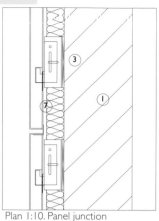

Plan 1:10. Panel junction

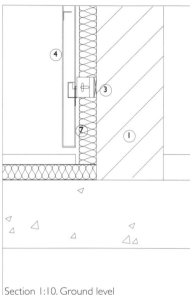

Section 1:10. Ground level

Bridgewatchers House, Rotterdam, Holland.
Architect: Architekturbüro Bolles + Wilson.

Section 1:10. Parapet and junction with ground slab

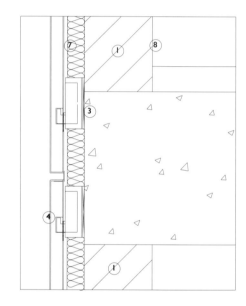

A much wider range of materials is used in rainscreens than was the case five years ago. Copper and zinc have the advantage of being easier to form than steel or aluminium, particularly where site-based construction methods are preferred for either economy or in dealing with complex or curved geometries. This method of fixing rainscreens avoids the need for off-site fabrication of a large number of different panel types with different curved geometries. They can be made economically on-site.

The 'tiling' or 'shingling' of panels in copper has been developed from sheet metal cladding. This departs from metal rainscreen designs in that the surface appearance has a deliberately uneven texture that emphasises the oil-canning effect that gives the appearance of a layered, tiled surface. The move away from the emphasis on flat metal panels in rainscreen construction includes an increased use of profiled and curved metal panels. A major advantage is that fixings can be concealed by semi-interlocking panels in the manner of sheet metal cladding or in the manner of traditional roof coverings.

There has been a recent increased use of semi-lapped assemblies that conceal the void behind the metal cladding. These usually have visible fixings at panel joints but allow the joints between panels to be less in shadow than is the case with other fixing methods. There has been a gradual development of rainscreens as visual screens rather than as weather-excluding panels. For example, perforated metal screens in mild steel or aluminium are used to create both modelling to a facade and solar shading set forward of glazed walling. In such designs the back of the rainscreen panel is visually as important as the outer visible face where the panel is seen through glazed openings in a facade. Fixings for such rainscreen panels often have screws and bolts that are set into the fixing rather than having projecting threaded bolt and exposed nuts.

Isometric view of wall assembly. TYPE 3

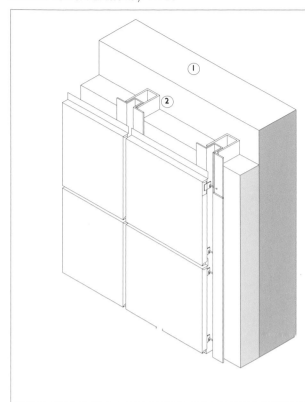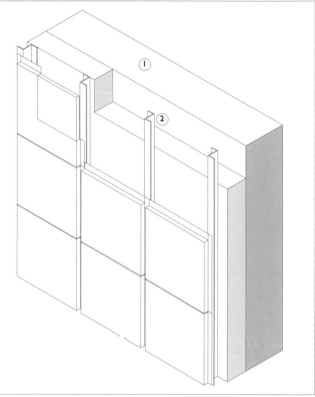

Details

1.	Backing wall or structural wall supporting rainscreen
2.	Support frame
3.	Support bracket

4. Metal rainscreen panel
5. Open joint
6. Closed cell thermal insulation
7. Waterproof membrane
8. Internal finish
9. Window frame inserted into

opening in backing wall or structural wall
10. Pressed metal cill
11. Pressed metal coping
12. Continuity of waterproofing layers of wall and roof

Section 1:10. Ground level

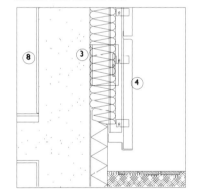

Plan 1:10. External corner

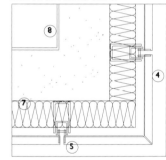

Plan 1:10. Internal corner with joint at corner

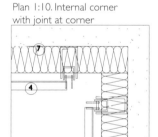

Plan 1:10. Internal corner with joints away from corner

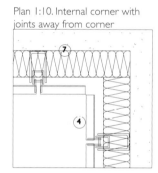

Materials

Rainscreen panels can have a flatness that is difficult to achieve with other methods. Panel flatness is achieved by either use of composites such as proprietary laminates where two sheets of aluminium are bonded on both sides of an inner core sheet of plastic of thickness 3-5mm (0.118in to 0.2in) or by a minimum 3mm (0.118in) thick aluminium sheet, or approximately 1mm thick steel sheet, depending on panel size. Honeycomb panels are also being used. A metal honeycomb layer, about 5mm (0.2in) thick, is bonded to thin metal sheets bonded on either side. Aluminium is most commonly used. One of the outer sheets is factory

paint coated from the rolled coil from which it is cut, giving the material a high level of colour consistency over large areas of panel.

Fixing methods

The three main fixing types used for metal rainscreens are (1) visible point fixed, (2) horizontal or vertical rails with partially exposed brackets (hung panels) and (3) vertical and horizontal rails with partially interlocking panels and concealed fixings.

The choice of fixing method is often determined by what is seen through the joint from the outside. If dark shadows are sought at the joint then the backing wall should have a consistent dark colour. In this

case, short lengths of bracket may be sufficient to support the panels, since they will not be visible. If the backing wall is likely to be visible through the open joints, such as if the backing wall is clad in exposed polystyrene insulation board, then the joints will need to be screened by a continuous channel.

Type (1) panels which are point fixed have either countersunk screws set flush with the panel face, or dome headed screws which make a visible feature of them. The screws are fixed into rails set to suit their position. Vertical rails are often preferred since water can easily drain down them.

Type (2) hung panels are hooked onto

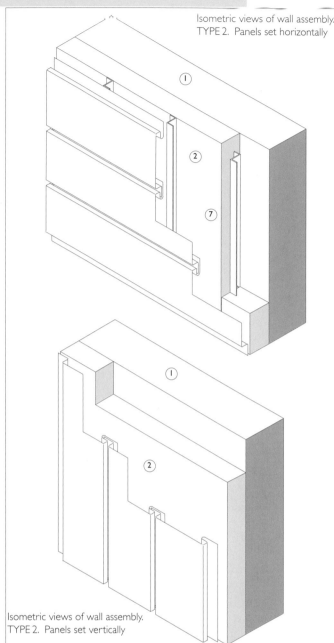

Isometric views of wall assembly.
TYPE 2. Panels set horizontally

Isometric views of wall assembly.
TYPE 2. Panels set vertically

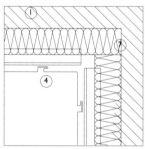

Bridgewatchers House, Rotterdam, Holland.
Architect: Architekturbüro Bolles + Wilson.

Details

1. Backing wall or structural wall sup
    porting rainscreen
2. Support frame
3. Support bracket
4. Metal rainscreen panel
5. Open joint
6. Closed cell thermal insulation
7. Waterproof membrane
8. Internal finish
9. Window frame inserted into open
    ing in backing wall or structural wall
10. Pressed metal cill
11. Pressed metal coping
12. Continuity of waterproofing layers of
    wall and roof

Plan 1:10. Internal corner

supporting brackets. Panels are fixed by cutting slots into the sides of the rainscreen panel during manufacture and hooking them onto dowels projecting from C-shaped brackets. These brackets are in turn secured to vertical rails set at vertical joints between panels. The rails also act as screens to close off views into the cavity. Horizontal joints are formed by an upstand formed in the top or bottom edge of a panel.

Type (3) semi-interlocking panels are fixed by screwing the top of the panel to horizontal rails to suit the orientation of the panels. The adjacent panel is lapped into the panel next to it, both to secure it and conceal the fixing. The joint in the other direction

is either fixed with a similar semi-interlocking edge to form a tiled appearance, or has a cover strip.

Unlike masonry-based rainscreens such as terracotta or stone, metal rainscreen panels are lightweight in comparison and need to be mechanically fixed at a minimum of one or two points, usually at the bottom of the panel if the panel is hung from the top. Fixing screws are usually applied at the joint, unless it is fixed with exposed fixings through the panel itself. This means that part of the bracket is usually visible. Short lengths of brackets then become visible and need to be incorporated as a visible part of the design.

Backing walls

Supporting walls to rainscreen panels are usually concrete block, which allows supporting panels to be fixed at any point across its surface, or framed, where rainscreen fixings are secured to the framing members rather than the outer skin of the backing wall. In some cases, if the outer skin is thick enough, say 6mm (0.25in) aluminium sheet, rainscreens can be fixed directly to the sheet material rather than the frame. Where a lightweight backing wall cannot accept additional loads from rainscreen cladding onto it (as with composite panels), then support rails span from floor to floor as posts.

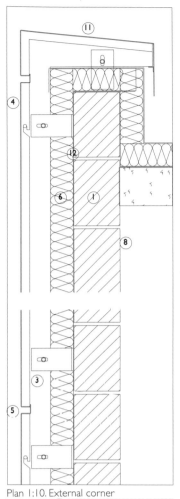

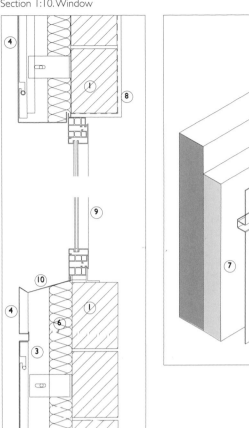

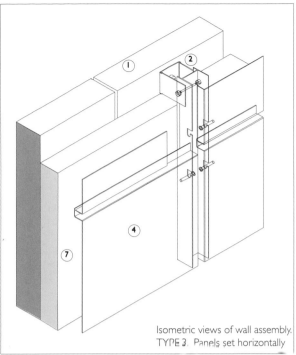

Isometric views of wall assembly.
TYPE 3. Panels set horizontally

Plan 1:10. External corner

Plan 1:10. External corner and window jamb

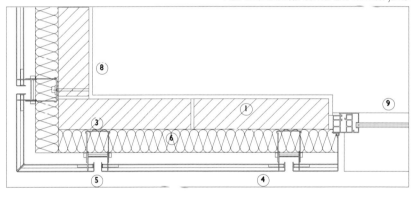

With concrete block backing walls, the thermal insulation is usually set on the outside face in order to keep the structure either warm or cool, depending on geographical location. The waterproof layer is set directly on the outside face of the concrete. The thermal insulation used is closed cell type in order for it not to absorb water which would drastically reduce its performance. The insulation is also used to protect the waterproof membrane but this makes it necessary for support brackets to be fixed through the insulation to the supporting wall behind. Sometimes holes have to be cut in the insulation, which reduces its effectiveness, but it is always better if the fixings for

support rails can be fixed at the same time as the insulation in order to co-ordinate them and avoid later cutting of the insulation.

With lightweight backing walls in timber or pressed steel, thermal insulation is set within the frame. A waterproofing layer is set on the inside (warm in winter) face. An internal finish layer is then set in front of this vapour barrier. Rainscreen fixings for support rails are fixed directly to the outer waterproofing layer using sealing washers that avoid leaks through the fixing point. The framed backing wall is designed to receive fixing brackets at points which transfer loads down to the primary structure. The use of

framed backing walls with rainscreens makes it necessary to co-ordinate the two elements of construction during the design rather than during the construction.

Construction sequence

An essential aspect of rainscreen construction is the sequence in which the various elements of the backing walls, windows, thermal insulation, waterproofing layer and rainscreen panel are brought together. Although the rainscreen principle is very effective and often very economic, its effectiveness can be reduced if seals are not properly applied or insulation is damaged because elements are assembled on site in the wrong order. Typi-

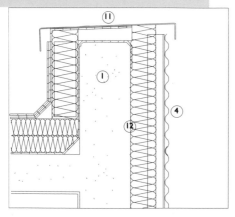

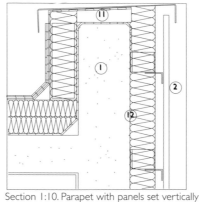

Section 1:10. Parapet and cill at ground level
with panels set horizontally

Section 1:10. Parapet with panels set vertically

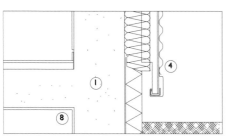

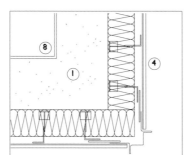

Plan 1:10. External corner

Section 1:10. Cill at ground level with panels
set vertically

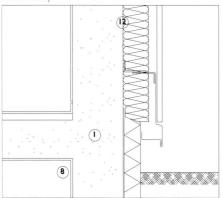

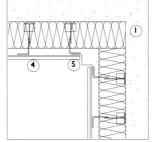

Plan 1:10. Internal corner

Isometric views of wall assembly.
TYPE 1 Panels set horizontally

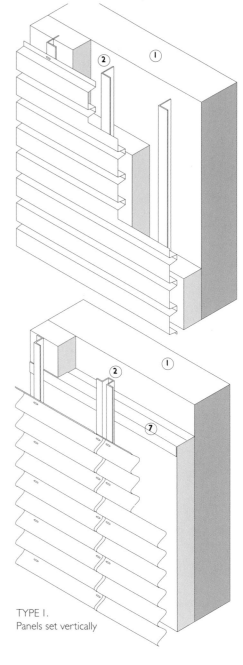

TYPE 1.
Panels set vertically

cally, windows are sealed against the backing wall before the rainscreen panels are set in place. An advantage of this form of construction is that the external wall can be made waterproof before the rainscreen panels are fixed.

A typical construction sequence is to build the backing wall first and set the waterproofing layer and insulation in place. Windows are then set into the backing wall and are sealed against its waterproofing layer. Thermal insulation, if set outside the line of the waterproofing layer (as in in-situ concrete, precast concrete or concrete block) makes it easier to set the thermal insulation on the backing wall after the windows and

doors have been fixed. Support rails for the rainscreen panels are then fixed to the backing wall, followed by the metal panels themselves. Panels are usually fixed in horizontal rows from the bottom up so that corner panels and panels at window openings can be fixed from the outside from the top of the panel. Metal panels can then be set in a correct alignment with the windows in terms of their position and in setting the required joint width. The open jointed nature of the construction usually dictates that the rainscreen panel is set in a way that avoids a view through the joint to the backing wall beyond.

Window and door openings

Because window and door openings are usually set into an opening before the rainscreen panels are set, reveals are sealed with either individual rainscreen panels or with sheet metal trims similar to those used for sheet metal construction. Unlike sheet metal construction however, a gap is usually maintained between the trim and the window in order to maintain the joint principle. Similarly gaps between reveal trims and adjacent wall panels are also separated by an open joint. Since windows and doors are sealed against the waterproofing layer behind the rainscreen panel rather than to the panel itself, these separations are straightforward to

Isometric views of wall assembly.

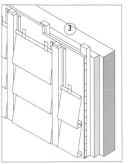

Plan 1:10. Internal corner

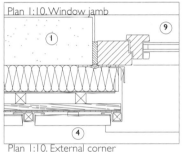

Plan 1:10. Window jamb

Plan 1:10. External corner

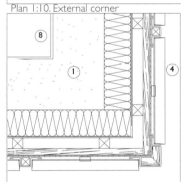

Section 1:10. Cill at ground level

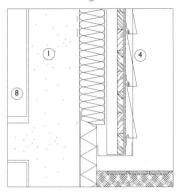

Section 1:10. Parapet

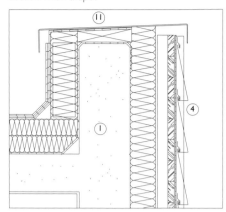

Details

1. Backing wall or structural wall supporting rainscreen
2. Support frame
3. Support bracket
4. Metal rainscreen panel
5. Open joint
6. Closed cell thermal insulation
7. Waterproof membrane
8. Internal finish
9. Window frame inserted into opening in backing wall or structural wall
10. Pressed metal cill
11. Pressed metal coping
12. Continuity of waterproofing layers of wall and roof

Bridgewatchers House, Rotterdam, Holland. Architect: Architekturburo Bolles + Wilson.

Section 1:10. Window

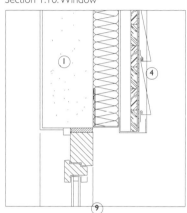

achieve. These open joints around openings are made in a way that conceals the waterproof layer behind, thus protecting it from both accidental damage from building users and from the possible effects from sunlight heating up the membrane or attacking it with UV light. Windows and doors are usually provided with an additional wider frame or trim at their edges in order to allow thermal insulation in the cavity to provide continuity at the opening and allow the rainscreen panel to lap against it.

Parapets and cills

Parapets have an open joint between the parapet flashing and the panel below but horizontal joints between flashings are usually closed to protect the parapet from accidental damage to the waterproofing undercloak beneath or from the harmful effects of sunlight from above acting on its horizontal surface. Joints between flashings may be recessed to match the visual appearance of the rainscreen panels by providing a shadow or may be lapped in the manner of fully supported sheet metal cladding. The waterproofing layer will form a continuous seal with the adjacent roofing membrane. Cills at the base of the wall are detailed in a similar way with metal being continuous but with joints either recessed or lapped.

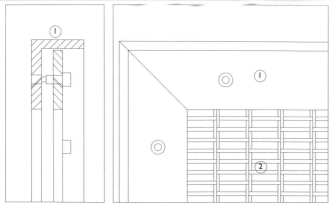

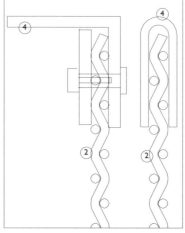

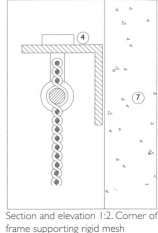

Section and elevation 1:2. Edge of frame supporting rigid mesh

Section and elevation 1:2. Corner of frame supporting rigid mesh

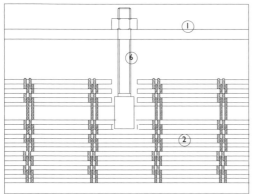

Section & elevation. 1:2 scale

Edge of support for mesh flexible in one direction. 1:2 scale

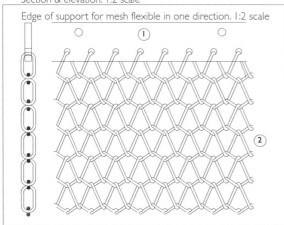

Kew House, Melbourne, Australia. Architect: Sean Godsell Architects.

Stainless steel mesh screens have been introduced into mainstream building construction only in the last ten years. This metal is preferred for mesh screens due to its durability and weather resistance when used externally. Their appearance as a textile rather than as a sheet material has led to the use of mesh as 'wraps' to facades in a similar way, in visual terms, to rainscreens. Their purpose is often to provide a smooth, textile-like surface across a wall that can conceal a variety of different facade elements immediately behind it. It has also found favour in car park design, where open mesh decks are given homogeneity with a woven mesh screen. Their varying levels of translucency can be exploit-

ed both in daylight by providing depth to a facade that gives some privacy to building users, and from a night time glow across its surface generated by electrical light within the building.

Meshes are of three essential types: rigid mesh made from rod, mesh flexible in one direction made as woven wire with rods in one direction and wire in the opposite direction, and mesh which is flexible in two directions which is made from woven wire only.

Rigid mesh

Rigid mesh is made in relatively small sheet sizes and is suitable mainly for balustrades or

areas of facades where the material can be supported on a visible frame. It is also used as external solar shading where its lightness in weight allows it to be moved in a motorised system. The material is made in both mild steel and stainless steel but mild steel requires painting. Polyester powder coating is the most common finish. Rigid mesh cannot be tensioned and so it is clamped in a frame at its edges.

This material is usually made in relatively small panels of around 1800 x 1500mm (6ft x 5ft). Stainless steel bars are woven in two directions, giving the material a stiffness comparable to aluminium sheet but with a surface texture much more undulating than

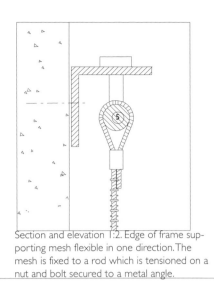

Section and elevation 1:2. Edge of frame supporting mesh flexible in one direction. The mesh is fixed to a rod which is tensioned on a nut and bolt secured to a metal angle.

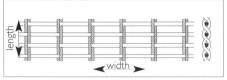

Mesh patterns which are flexible in one direction. 1:2 scale

Details for mesh
1. Metal support edge frame
2. Stainless steel mesh
3. Stainless steel spring
4. Metal fixing bracket
5. Metal support rod
6. Fixing bolt to tension mesh
7. Floor slab or backing wall
8. Adjacent curtain wall

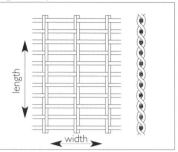

Rigid mesh pattern. 1:2 scale

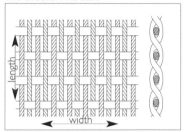

Mesh patterns which are flexible in one direction. 1:2 scale

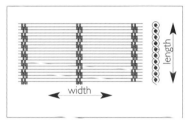

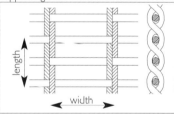

Section and elevation 1:2. Edge of frame supporting mesh flexible in one direction.

The mesh is fixed to patch fittings which are tensioned by springs. The springs are supported by a carrier frame.

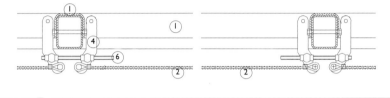

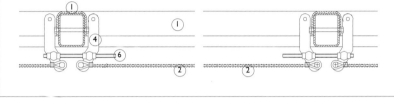

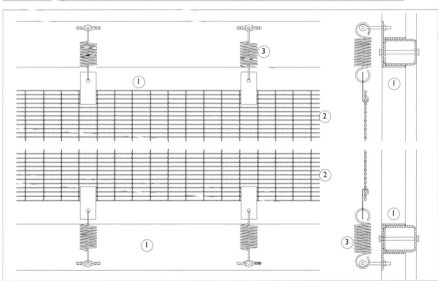

perforated metal sheet. Rigid mesh can provide up to around 50% shading. Rod thickness is typically 1.5mm (0.054in) diameter woven to form openings of around 6mm × 2mm (0.25in × 0.08in). Because they cannot be tensioned, rigid meshes are either held in a continuous edge frame or supported at points in the manner of bolt fixed glazing. They are most commonly used in balustrading where rigidity of material is an essential requirement. The economic nature of the material allows it to be used as both balustrading and full height screening as part of the same design. When used as a balustrade, the exposed edges of the material are held captive in a protective edging if

not fixed into a full supporting frame. This avoids injury to building users. A folded flat sheet or a pair of flats are commonly used.

Meshes flexible in one direction
These meshes are made with rigid stainless steel rod in one direction woven and stainless steel cable in the other direction. An advantage presented by the cables is that they can be tensioned at each end to provide a large continuous flat area of translucent metal.

Most of these meshes come in a maximum width of around 7500mm (25ft). Since the material is made as a continuous run, it

can be made in very long lengths, making it ideal for use in a single run of material from top to bottom of a facade without joints. In terms of transparency, the material can vary from around 25% light transmission to 65% depending on the weave. The amount of light transmission can be varied by increasing the thickness and frequency of cables. The distance between rods cannot be varied by reducing the thickness of the cable, allowing it to be more tightly woven, but more cables are usually introduced to compensate for the loss of strength in the cable when tensioned. Cable thickness can vary from 2.0mm to 2.5mm (0.08in to 0.1in) diameter. Rod thicknesses can vary from 2.0mm

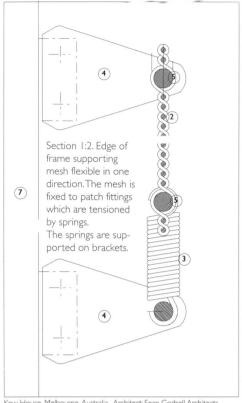

Section 1:2. Edge of frame supporting mesh flexible in one direction. The mesh is fixed to patch fittings which are tensioned by springs. The springs are supported on brackets.

Kew House, Melbourne, Australia. Architect: Sean Godsell Architects.

Section and elevation 1:2. Edge of frame supporting mesh flexible in one direction. The mesh is fixed to a rod which is tensioned on a nut and bolt secured to a metal angle.

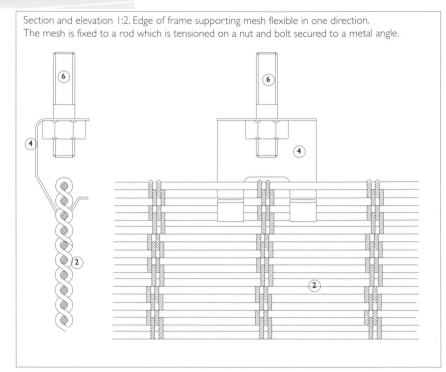

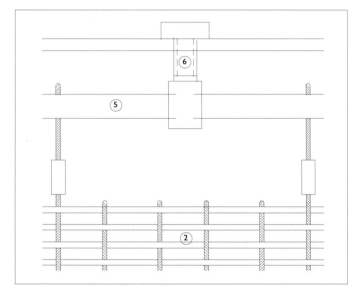

(0.08in) up to 4mm (0.15in) diameter. The weave pattern can vary from 4mm x 10mm (0.18in x 0.37in) to 4mm x 100mm (0.18in x 4in), giving very different visual effects from dense to very open. In addition, varying densities can be woven into a single panel, or length, of material.

Meshes flexible in one direction are fixed by tensioning the cables at each end. The cable is usually set vertically to avoid sag associated with horizontal laying. The cables are looped in a secure loop at each end around a rod or bar. One end is fixed while the other is tensioned by springs set at intervals along the length of the horizontal bar. Springs are usually set at the bottom so that

the mesh is first hung, then secured and tensioned at the bottom. Lateral stability to the mesh over a long run of the material is provided either by bars woven or fixed into the mesh, or by point fixings. The point fixings comprise discs set either side of the mesh to hold the material in place. A bolt runs through an opening in the mesh between the two discs, which is secured back to the supporting structure, typically a floor slab or backing wall. Meshes will span 2.0 to 2.5 metres (6ft 6in to 8ft) vertically between points of lateral restraint. Adjacent sheets can be fixed together by using a bracket with two bolts in the manner of bolt fixed glazing or by lapping the mesh panels and using a

single bolt in the manner of a popper on textile cloths as used in denim jeans, for example. Applications of mesh using wide strips are increasingly common, in widths from 5 to 7metres, (16ft to 23ft) hung from continuous rods and restrained back to a frame at 1.0 to 1.5 metre (3ft 3in to 5ft) centres.

Fully flexible mesh

This material is made as a woven-wire cloth or as a crimped wire panel. Wires are crimped down the length of the material and straight wires across its width. The woven cloth type is manufactured primarily for small solar shading screens. It is also used

Section 1:10. Parapet of perforated metal screen..

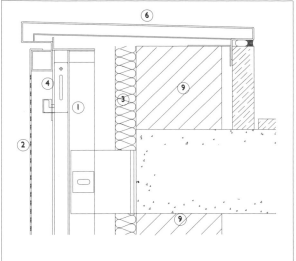

Kew House, Melbourne, Australia. Architect: Sean Godsell Architects.

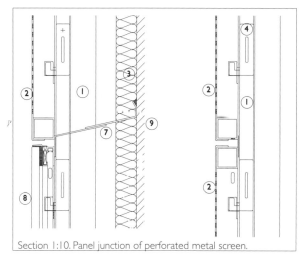

Plan 1:10. External corner of perforated metal screen.

Section 1:10. Panel junction of perforated metal screen.

Details for perforated metal

1. Metal support frame
2. Perforated metal sheet
3. Thermal insulation
4. Metal fixing bracket
5. Fixing bolt
6. Pressed metal parapet coping
7. Cavity tray
8. Adjacent glazing
9. Backing wall

for balustrades in continuous long lengths and as vertically- or horizontally-set bands of solar shading material. Large panels are not interrupted by joint lines. The material is fixed by tensioning it vertically. Closely woven meshes have a light transmission of between 1% and 5%, while crimped wire screens vary from 25% to 50%. The tightly woven types are made in widths from around 1800mm to 2400mm (6ft to 8ft) and are made in very long lengths. The more open weaves have an appearance similar to those with cables, using straight rod in one direction, weaving rod in the other direction around the flat rod. These open weave types are made in widths of around 6000mm

(20ft) though these sizes are difficult to use in facade panels since the support grid of around 2000mm (6ft 6in) is usually needed to restrain the material. Since the material is made from rod, metals other than stainless steel can be used, though typically copper and bronze are the most common alternatives. They are less rigid than stainless steel but can produce quite dramatic visual effects. A grid of 3mm x 1.5mm (0.125in x 0.0625in) is common in this more open weave material.

Mesh used on curves

Regular mesh that is rigid in one direction is difficult to curve, as it is suited to flat, rectilin-

ear designs. Curves can be formed over lengths of 2-3 metres (6ft 6in to 10ft) by setting out the cables on a curve top and bottom which forces the thin rods in the opposite direction to the curve. However, meshes are being developed which can take up curves more easily for complex geometries. Instead of using cables, loops of stainless steel strip are woven in loops between rows of rods. This allows the rods to be bent around a form or bowed out by brackets, while allowing the loops to be individually stretched between each row of rods. Variations on this type of mesh are set to grow over the next 10 years.

Section and elevations 1:25. Edge of frame supporting mesh
flexible in one direction. The mesh is fixed to patch fittings which are
tensioned by springs. The springs are supported on brackets.

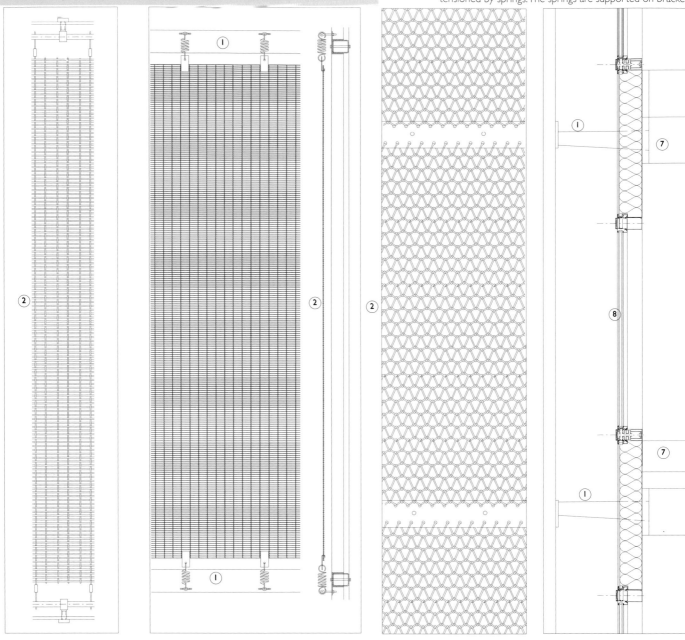

Perforated metal

Non-rectilinear or irregular geometric shapes
in flat or curved form can more easily be
achieved in perforated metal. Although panel
sizes are much smaller than tensioned mesh,
a greater range of forms can currently be
made more economically. Perforated metal in
each mild steel (paint or polyester powder
coated) and aluminium (polyester powder
coated or PVDF coated) are used. Both
materials are manufactured with perforations
of different shapes and percentages of perforations. Circular holes are the most commonly used as they are straightforward to manufacture. They are also able to have a closely
controlled percentage of perforation by vary-

ing both the size of the holes and their prox-
imity. This makes the material very useful if a
precise shading coefficient (percentage of
solar shading) or light transmission is speci-
fied for a facade. By varying both the hole
diameter and the centres of the holes, different visual effects of transparency can be
achieved. Squares and various decorative
motifs are also made but with less control
on precise perforation percentages.

Steel and aluminium sheet are commonly available in sizes up to around 3 metres ×
2.5 metres (10ft × 8ft) in 3mm (0.118in)
thick sheet allowing panels to be reasonably
large, depending on wind load considerations. In general, the higher the percentage of

perforation, the lower the wind load on the
perforated metal panel. Perforated metal
panels are usually fixed back to an edge
frame made from angle or profile in the
same material. The edges of the metal are
usually not perforated in order to conceal
the frame behind. The increased use of
water jet cutting machines allows for a much
greater control of the extent of pattern on a
sheet. Perforated metal panels are then fixed
back to the primary structure with a variety
of hanging brackets, ties and struts to suit
the design. Supporting structure is visually
very refined if visible through the metal, particularly at night if the panel assembly is visible from lighting within the building. A series

Plan, section and elevation 1:25. Frame supporting rigid mesh. The mesh is fixed to a metal edge frame which is supported by brackets.

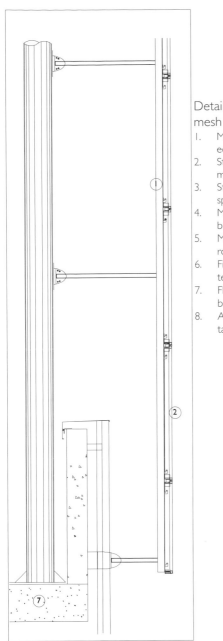

Details for mesh

1. Metal support edge frame
2. Stainless steel mesh
3. Stainless steel spring
4. Metal fixing bracket
5. Metal support rod
6. Fixing bolt to tension mesh
7. Floor slab or backing wall
8. Adjacent curtain wall

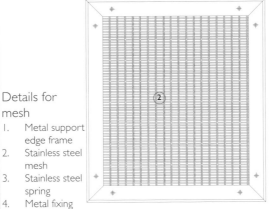

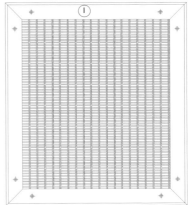

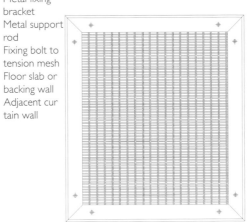

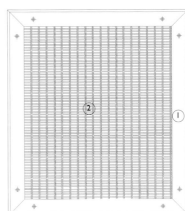

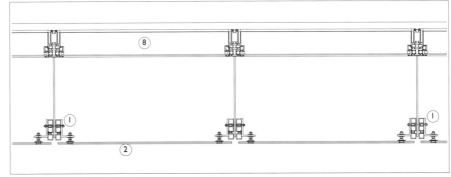

of forked pin connections or cast moment connectors are increasingly being used, with tapered tubular framing members or box sections with complex sections increasingly the norm. Because the metal framing is exposed to the effects of weather, a high specification paint is used for steel, and either polyester powder coating or PVDF coatings are used for aluminium. Anodising has become more popular in recent years but requires very close control in the factory to avoid visible colour differences between adjacent anodised panels.

Kew House, Melbourne, Australia. Architect: Sean Godsell Architects.

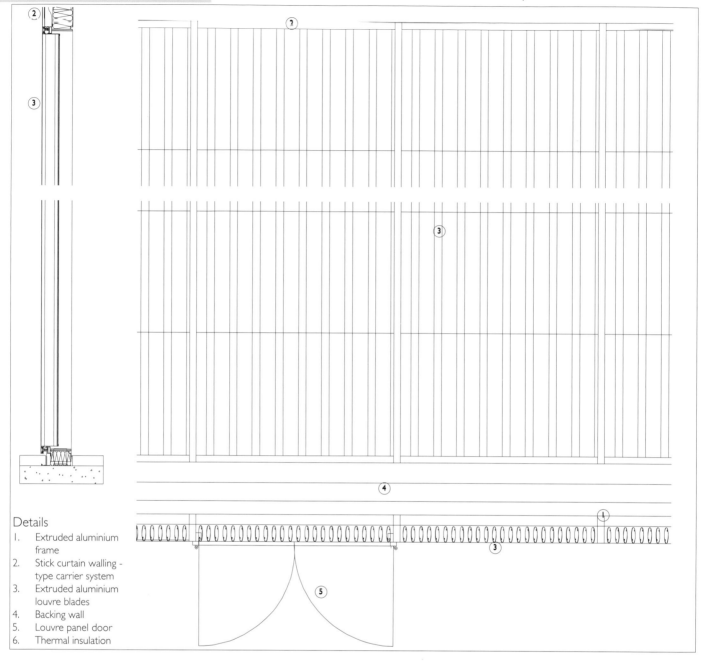

Details

1. Extruded aluminium frame
2. Stick curtain walling - type carrier system
3. Extruded aluminium louvre blades
4. Backing wall
5. Louvre panel door
6. Thermal insulation

Metal louvres are typically used for two purposes: as weather-resisting screens to naturally ventilated spaces such as plant rooms, as terminations to the ends of air-handling ducts where they penetrate the external wall, or alternatively as solar shading on the outside of facades in front of glazed walls or windows. Glazed louvres are also used to provide natural ventilation to winter garden spaces where they also provide light, as in high level clerestorey glazing or in glazed walls in winter gardens in housing. Glass louvres are generally adjustable. Metal louvres are used for air handling ducts or plant rooms, and can be in single, double or triple bank depending on the amount of weather resistance required.

MCF_ 58

Metal louvres

Louvre panels can be set either horizontally or vertically. Horizontal louvres have inclined blades set in extruded aluminium set in a frame of the same material. Some louvres throw the water clear of the edge of the blade at the front. Others where more weather protection is needed, have either a drainage channel at the front, or are made as a V-shape in order to drain water away into the sides of the frame where it is ejected to the outside at the cill. Open gauge mesh is usually set at the back of the louvre panel to prevent the passage of birds. Louvres without drainage channels are used in sheltered areas and also where rain that is blown through the louvre will not damage the

building fabric. Drained louvres are used where more weather protection is needed, usually where exposure to the weather is more severe and where water penetration through the panel must be reduced. These drained louvres allow a little less air movement than the standard types, and more louvre area is usually provided to compensate for this. The use of a double bank louvre ensures that water blown over the top of the outer blade will run down the face of the inner blade and be drained away. The free area from the louvres is around 50%.

Horizontally-set blades are set 50mm apart. Stiffener bars are set at centres from 1000mm (3ft 3in) to 1500mm (5ft) vertical centres, depending on blade size and materi-

Plan 1:10. Corners of vertically-set extruded aluminium louvres

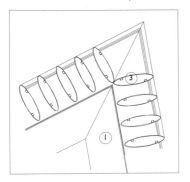
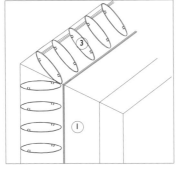

Plan 1:10. Vertically-set extruded aluminium louvres. Panel to panel junction and panel to door junction

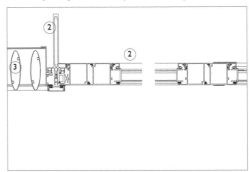

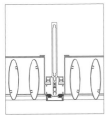

British School in the Netherlands, The Hague, Holland. Architect: Kraaijvanger Urbis.

Section 1:10. Louvred door

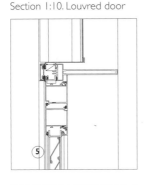

Section 1:10. Vertically-set extruded aluminium louvres

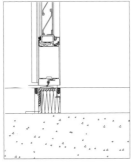

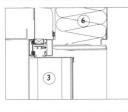

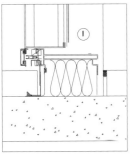

al thickness. These bars are not visible directly from the outside but can be seen from below if louvres are set at an angle that allows views through them. Louvre blades are fixed to the stiffeners with extruded aluminium clips to stiffen the blades. Corners of frames to louvre panels are mitred and screwed or welded. The edge has different profiles to suit being glazed into adjacent curtain walling, and has either recessed joints between panels, or a wide frame, to suit the type of additional support needed for the complete louvred panel width.

Vertically-set louvres have blades set at an angle (in plan) such that water drains down the face of the louvres and is drained away at the bottom of the frame. They are

deeper than the simplest horizontal types and perform in a similar way to the drained horizontal types. Their depth also ensures that views through the louvre panels are severely reduced. Profiles for vertical louvres can be both V-shaped and elliptical. The free area is also around 50%. Panels are assembled in a factory for coupling together on site. Typical panel sizes are around 1.5 metres × 2.5 metres (5ft × 8ft) for both vertical and horizontally set louvres. Larger panels can be fabricated, but transportation to site becomes more difficult. Louvred panels can be arranged in heights up to around 4 metres (13ft) with extruded aluminium mullions. Above this height, additional steel posts are required behind panel joints to provide

both support and lateral restraint.

Louvre panels can also be set at inclined angles but resistance to rain penetration is significantly reduced on inclined walls that can be seen from below. Louvres can be set upside down to avoid views through the screen, but they provide no weather protection. In both cases, an additional vertical louvre is set behind to exclude rain.

Banks of louvre blades can also be made to tilt to suit varying ventilation requirements, such as in buildings with a high degree of natural ventilation. Panels can open and close from rain and wind sensors forming part of the BMS (building management system). Panel sizes are similar to those of fixed panels, that is, 1.5 × 2.5 metres (5ft ×

Section 1.10. Typical louvred solar shading canopies

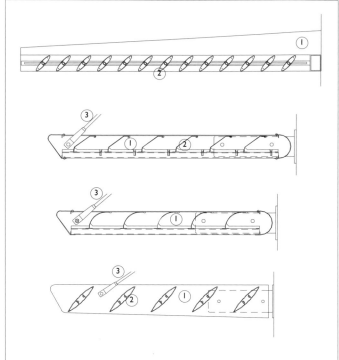

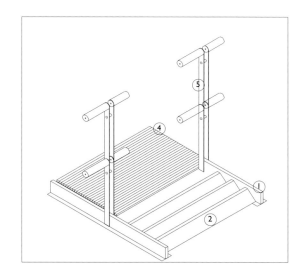

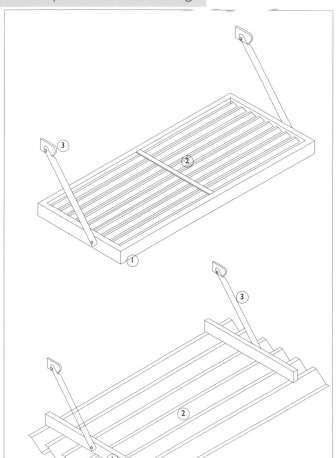

Isometric view of assembly. Typical louvred solar shading canopies

Details for canopies

1. Metal support frame
2. Extruded aluminium louvre blades
3. Supporting rods or tubes
4. Extruded aluminium decking for maintenance
5. Balustrade

8ft). They have a single rod set into the edge frame which connects all the blades together and which is pushed up and down by a separate motor or is connected to a manual winding rod.

Doors are made in the same way as louvre panels but have stiffer frames to suit movement. They are designed with louvre panels and are often the same size in order to conceal their appearance.

Sandtrap louvres are designed for use in sandy and dusty conditions to prevent most airborne sand and dust from passing through the louvre. They consist of vertically-set C-shaped aluminium profiles which interlock to provide a continuous barrier. Air passing through the louvre passes round the inter-

locking profiles while sand is trapped by the inner profile and falls to the bottom of the frame. The cill is inclined to ensure that sand falls out of the bottom of the panel at the front. Sandtrap louvres remove most of the sand and dust particles before the air reaches the filters on mechanical ventilation equipment. Insect screen is also usually provided and this has little effect on air flow rates. Maximum sizes are similar to those of other louvre types in 1.5 × 2.0 metres (5ft × 6ft 6in), though as with all louvre types, larger panels can be specially made.

Glazed louvres

These have traditionally been poor excluders of air (high air infiltration rates) but they

have improved significantly in recent years. The amount of opening can be closely controlled. They consist of glass blades held in an aluminium frame or in aluminium clips, secured on pivots into an edge frame made from extruded aluminium profiles. Some clips holding the glass in place are made from polypropylene rather than aluminium, to avoid rattling between the two components. The most recent development has been in thin aluminium clips and the use of bolt fixed glazing to hold the glass in place.

Louvre glass blades are usually made in laminated glass for safety, though float glass is sometimes used for small-scale applications. Solar control glasses are often used to match adjacent areas of glazing. Single or

Section 1:10. Horizontally-set extruded aluminium louvres

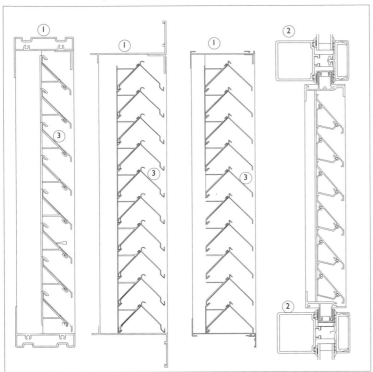

British School in the Netherlands, The Hague, Holland. Architect: Kraaijvanger Urbis.

Plan 1:10 Typical extruded solar shading louvre sections

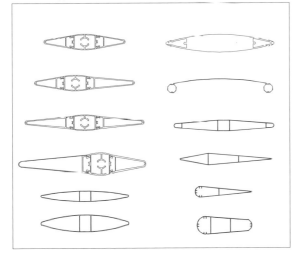

Details

1. Extruded aluminium frame
2. Stick curtain walling - type carrier system
3. Extruded aluminium louvre blades
4. Backing wall
5. Louvre panel door
6. Thermal insulation

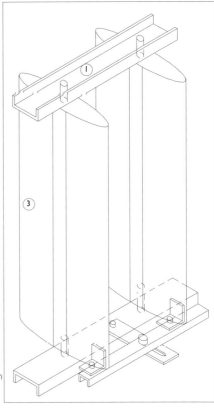

Isometric view of assembly. Vertically-set pivoted louvres with sliding movement mechanism

double glazed units are available. Glass louvre panels are either hand operated by a wire cable-type winding handle or are electrically operated with rods as used in metal louvres. Electrically operated units are generally 1500mm (5ft) high to suit the length of the rods. Panels are coupled vertically or horizontally to form a large-scale screen of panels. They can also be glazed into curtain walling systems. Maximum sizes are bigger than metal louvres in 2400mm × 2400mm (8ft × 8ft) approximately, but maximum length of ventilator unit is around 1200mm (4ft). Automatic opening types are used as smoke vents in the event of fire. They provide around 70% free area when fully open.

Where double glazed units are used,

they are typically in 24mm thick overall units of 4/16/4 (glass/cavity/glass). The outer 4mm is slightly thicker if a laminated glass is used for safety. Like single glazed louvres, the maximum length of a panel is 1200mm (4ft), but two are commonly joined to provide an overall maximum panel length of 2400mm (8ft). The thicker frames give less free area for ventilation of around 50%. Although the glass is insulated for reasons of energy conservation, frames are not yet thermally broken. Condensation risk when windows are closed is assessed for each application.

Solar shading

Metal louvres are also used as solar shading on glazed facades. Louvres are located either

in panels set away from the external wall or horizontally projecting from the facade as cantilevered panels. Louvres are set either horizontally or vertically to suit the protection needed from varying sun angles. Vertically-set louvres are positioned forward of the glass, usually a minimum of 600mm (2ft) to allow a person to pass between the external wall and louvres for maintenance access and cleaning. The shading devices are fixed to vertical posts or mullions which usually coincide with the module of the glazing behind. Horizontally-set panels consist of fixed louvres, usually inclined at 45° to the vertical in order to maximise the shading effect. The louvres are fixed to mild steel channels or T-sections which are in turn fixed

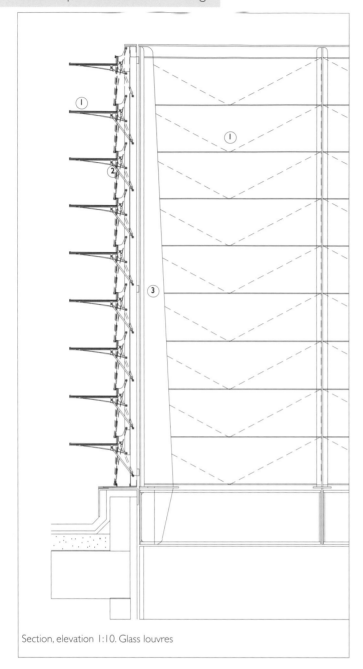

Section, elevation 1:10. Glass louvres

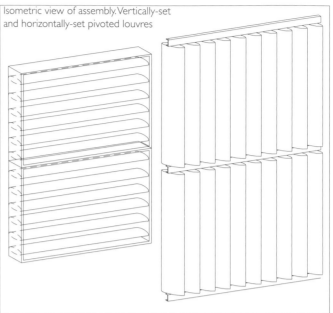

Isometric view of assembly. Vertically-set and horizontally-set pivoted louvres

British School in the Netherlands, The Hague, Holland. Architect: Kraaijvanger Urbis.

to support brackets projecting through the external wall. Where glazed curtain walling is used, the support bracket goes through the mullion (vertical member) where it can be properly sealed against water penetration. Louvres for both vertical and horizontal shading usually span much further than those used in 1200mm (4ft) wide opening louvre panels, and consequently need to be more rigid as a result. Panels project a maximum of around 1000mm (3ft 3in) without additional diagonal tie rods to prop the panels. Most proprietary systems can reach 2000mm (6ft 6in) with an additional diagonal brace.

Elliptical and aerofoil-shaped aluminium profiles are most commonly used since their shape is seen outside the building and from

inside. More traditional Z-shaped louvre profiles are also used. An advantage of horizontally-set louvres over projecting canopies is that they do not require rainwater drainage that is needed for a continuous horizontal surface. Small louvre blades are made as a single extrusion, but larger louvres, up to around 500mm (1ft 8in) in width are made from an extruded aluminium core to which curved or flat aluminium sections, usually 3mm (0.118in) thick, are fixed. The ends of profiles are fitted with extruded aluminium end caps both for visual reasons and to protect the inside surfaces from corrosion. Aluminium louvres are finished in either PVDF or polyester powder coating. Blades are usually fixed at their ends from the centre of the

extrusion at a single point at each end.

Where louvres are motorised, they are fixed at single pivot points to vertical posts. Link rods are set into the support post joining each blade in order to operate a set of louvres from a single motor. Pivots have nylon bushes fitted to avoid long term rattle and noise from the moving parts.

Vertically-set louvres use the same variety of section profiles and are set on transom (horizontal) sections that are connected back to mullions or directly back to the external wall. Vertical louvre sections using an elliptical or aerofoil profile can span up to around 3000mm (10ft) vertically without need for additional stiffeners.

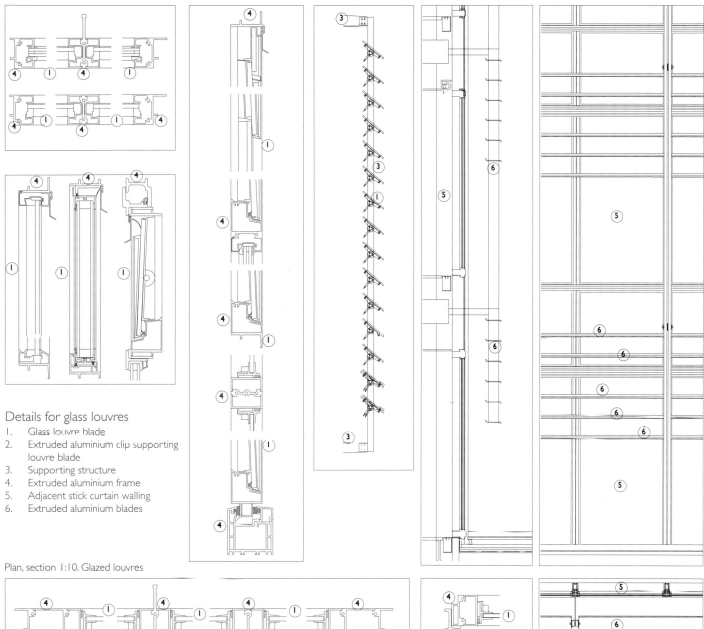

Details for glass louvres
1. Glass louvre blade
2. Extruded aluminium clip supporting louvre blade
3. Supporting structure
4. Extruded aluminium frame
5. Adjacent stick curtain walling
6. Extruded aluminium blades

Plan, section 1:10. Glazed louvres

Walkways

Horizontally-set louvres can also be used as maintenance walkways if they are made sufficiently rigid. T-section aluminium profiles are used, and have a serrated top to provide an anti-slip surface. A fall arrest system is used to secure maintenance personnel to the walkway. This consists of a continuous cable or tube fixed to a convenient point along the walkway. A maintenance person in a harness is then linked to the continuous cable or tube by a secure line. The aluminium T-sections are fixed to steel I-sections or channels which span between column supports adjacent to the external wall, typically at around 7500mm (24ft 6in) centres. The main sections supporting the T-sections are

fixed to stainless steel or aluminium brackets that project through the external wall from the edge of the floor slab.

A recent development in metal louvre design is in movable types. Louvres are set on a moving rack which allows them to be moved from open to closed, using perforated aluminium sheet to form louvres. When closed, the louvres create a translucent screen with 20% to 50% light transmission (depending on the degree of perforation in the steel) to 100% light transmission when open. This allows a glazed wall to deal with changing sun angles at different times of day and different times of year through a change in the angle of the blade only. This system is used on both vertical and horizontal planes,

for example on large glass facades as well as projecting areas of horizontal glazing within the facade. The use of more complex metal profiles where blades interlock, together with different perforated metals and their connection to a BMS (building management system) is sure to make significant developments over the next 10 years. Such controls can reduce energy consumption within a building by reducing the amount of mechanical cooling needed as well as control glare from direct sunlight.

2

GLASS

(1) **Stick glazing:**

System assembly

Framing profiles

Opening lights

Parapets, cills, penetrations

Corners

Spandrel panels

(2) **Unitised glazing:**

Jointing panels

Opening lights

Corner panels, parapets and cills

Silicone-bonded glazing

(3) **Clamped glazing:**

Patch plate glazing

Clamped glazing

Opaque glazing

(4) **Bolt fixed glazing:**

Support methods

Bottom supported glazing

Top hung glazing

Corners

Seals and interfaces

(5) **Glass blocks:**

Fixing glass blocks

Support frames and walls

Cast glass channels

(6) **Steel windows:**

Small-scale glazing

Large-scale glazing

(7) **Aluminium and PVC-U windows:**

Windows in openings

Window walls

Composite windows

(8) **Timber windows:**

Window walls

Window design

Windows in openings

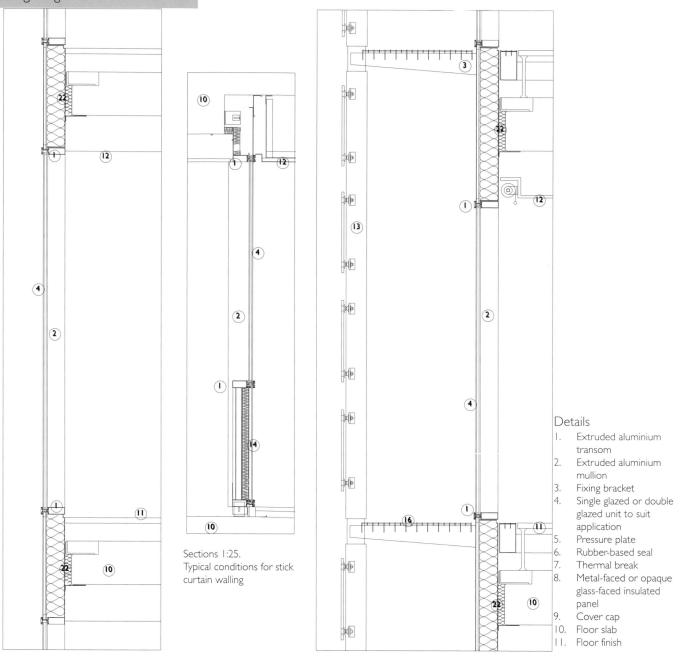

Sections 1:25.
Typical conditions for stick
curtain walling

Details
1.   Extruded aluminium
     transom
2.   Extruded aluminium
     mullion
3.   Fixing bracket
4.   Single glazed or double
     glazed unit to suit
     application
5.   Pressure plate
6.   Rubber-based seal
7.   Thermal break
8.   Metal-faced or opaque
     glass-faced insulated
     panel
9.   Cover cap
10. Floor slab
11. Floor finish

Comparison with unitised glazing

Framed glazing systems are of two types: stick and unitised. Stick systems are assembled mainly on site, while unitised systems are assembled in a factory. Stick systems are well adapted for non-modular construction. While unitised systems require a repetition in panel sizes in order to keep the types to a small number in order to remain economic, stick systems allow a high degree of freedom in module size and in facade design. Mullions and transoms do not need to be continuous; glazing bars can be set out in staggered grids and be changed easily from smaller grid sizes to larger ones. Complex geometries can be taken up much more easily by stick systems than by unitised systems. Stick systems are

often preferred for low rise building, where scaffolding is used, but the increased use of mast climbers (moving platforms) is making stick systems viable for taller buildings (10 to 20 storeys) where unitised glazing would otherwise have been used. The increased dependence on mast climbers is in part due to the need to be independent of site cranes, which are increasingly needed to service the construction of the primary structure often being built at the same time, though usually several floors higher or several bays away from the glazed walling.

For low rise building, or where there is a high degree of variation in the facade module, stick glazing is often preferred, since the

wall is assembled in place on site rather than in a workshop, making it very economic when compared to unitised glazing. Although off-site fabrication saves time and can be of higher quality, it is often more expensive. Sometimes mullions and transoms are preassembled into carrier frames that are lifted in place and fixed without glass. This 'semi-unitised' approach can save time on construction where there is some degree of repetition.

A criticism of stick systems has traditionally been of their poorer quality of assembly when compared to unitised glazing, but this is much less the case today. However, bringing all the components together at the site,

University Library, Delft, Holland. Architect: Mecanoo architekten bv.

Sections 1:5. Junctions between double glazed
units and the following: :
A.   Another double glazed unit
B.   Glass spandrel panel
C.   Metal honeycomb panel
D.   Inward opening window

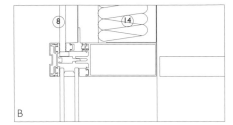

B

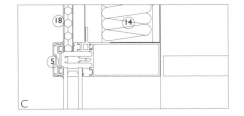

C

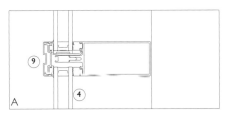

A

Section 1:5. Junction with edge of
floor slab

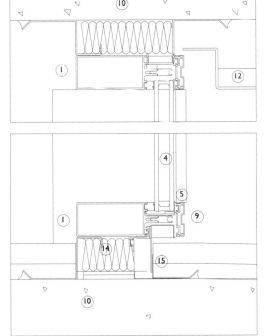

12.   Ceiling finish
13.   Outer glazed screen
        providing solar shading
14.   Thermal insulation
15.   Metal sheet seal
16.   Maintenance access deck
17.   Window glazed in
        curtain walling
18.   Metal honeycomb panel
19.   Slot in mullion to receive
        fixing bracket for
        external screens, etc.
20.   Steel hollow section
21.   Adjacent wall. Metal rain
        screen shown
22.   Smoke seal

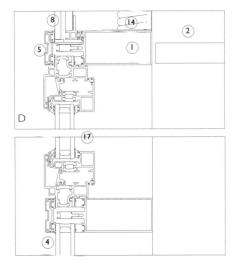

D

of double- or single-glazed units, aluminium profiles, rubber-based gaskets and seals, folded metal flashings and copings, involves a much higher dependence on site-based work to achieve the quality of construction of the factory-based unitised systems.

System assembly

An essential aspect of stick systems is that they should be drained and ventilated in order to avoid water being drawn through the rubber-based seals into the building. Rainwater penetrating the outer seal is drained away in a ventilated zone that provides pressure equalisation between outside and inside the system. Pressure equalisation avoids water being drawn into the system by a pres-

sure difference between two chambers, resulting in water being drawn through a joint. Any rainwater entering this zone is drained away to the outside forward of the inner seal forming a second line of defence against air and water infiltration. Most stick systems now provide a full thermal break through the aluminium profiles rather than the partial thermal breaks provided on previous systems. This reduces condensation risk on the inside face of the framing in temperate climates. In hot and humid climates, the condensation will occur harmlessly on the outside face of the framing if the interior is cooled by mechanical ventilation. In all climates, a thermal break improves the U-value of the glazed wall, thus reducing energy con-

sumption within the building for either heating or cooling.

Stick glazing is assembled mainly on site. Mullions (verticals) are fixed to floor slabs with transoms (horizontals) spanning between the mullions to which they are fixed. These framing members can be pre-assembled into 'ladders' on the ground and lifted into place by crane in order to reduce time on site. The glass is set in place and pressure plates fixed through thermal breaks back to the carrier frame of mullions and transoms. Decorative cappings are usually applied to the pressure plates to conceal the pressure plates as well as the self tapping screws holding the glass in place. Sometimes

Section 1:5. Stick curtain walling set
into a window opening

Sections 1:5. Junctions at base of wall

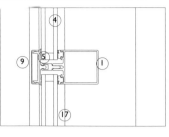

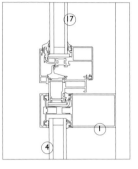

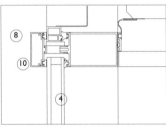

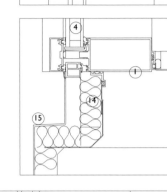

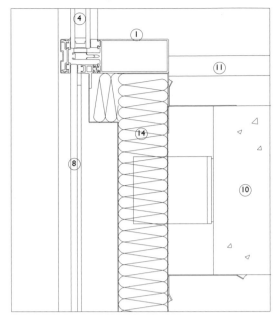

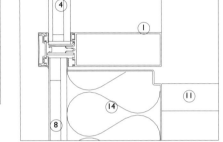

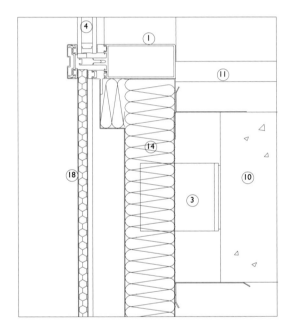

Sections 1:5

Details
1. Extruded aluminium transom
2. Extruded aluminium mullion
3. Fixing bracket
4. Single glazed or double glazed unit to suit application
5. Pressure plate
6. Rubber-based seal
7. Thermal break
8. Metal-faced or opaque glass-faced insulated panel
9. Cover cap
10. Floor slab

the cappings are omitted but care must be taken to ensure that the screws are properly aligned and that the pressure plates are continuous and jointed carefully.

Stick systems are fixed from floor to floor at either side of the floor slab or on top. The design of the connection is dependent mainly on the method of forming the edge of the floor construction on floor depths or uses of the adjacent floor zone, and any additional elements such as brackets for solar shading or maintenance walkways which penetrate the stick glazing. The glazing is either hung from each floor level or sits on each floor level. Hanging is usually preferred but constraints imposed by the structure of the

building may require the glazing to be supported at the base of each mullion. Mullions are linked by spigots so that the restrained end of one mullion fits into the supported end of the other mullion.

Because glazed walling is set forward of the edge of the slab, the gap between the two is closed with a floor finish. Seals between adjacent floors are designed as either smoke seals or as flame barriers. Smoke seals comprise a mineral wool or glass wool barrier, held in place and sealed with galvanised steel sheet above and below. Flame barriers, usually of one hour or 90 minute rating are provided by a specially protected spandrel panel at the level of the

floor zone. The spandrel panel forming the barrier is fixed directly to the floor slab as well as forming part of the curtain wall system. This ensures that the spandrel remains in place long after the adjacent curtain walling has collapsed during a fire. The spandrel panel itself is usually protected with a fire resistant board as part of the barrier.

Where glazing is inclined significantly from the vertical, two-edge glazing is used to allow the water to run down unimpeded with transoms. This is a standard method for glazed roofs, where mullions are capped, but transoms running across the width of the slope are sealed with a flush silicone joint.

Plans 1:5

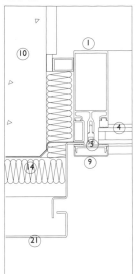
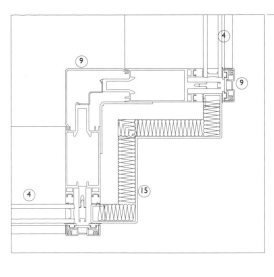
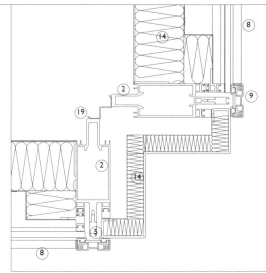

University Library, Delft, Holland. Architect: Mecanoo architekten bv.

11. Floor finish
12. Ceiling finish
13 Outer glazed screen providing solar shading
14. Thermal insulation
15. Metal sheet seal
16. Maintenance access deck
17. Window glazed in curtain walling

18. Metal honeycomb panel
19. Slot in mullion to receive fixing bracket for external screens, etc.
20. Steel hollow section wall
21. Adjacent metal rainscreen shown
22. Smoke seal

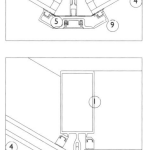
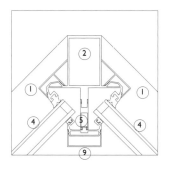

Framing profiles

Carrier frames are made from a wide variety of sections. The shape can usually be adapted for a specific project. The most common types are rectangular box sections that use the full width of the joint, and narrower T-shaped and I-shaped sections that are narrower than the joint width. Although the depth of the profile is determined by structural requirements, the overall shape can be adapted to suit other needs, such as incorporating roller blind guides into the sides of the vertical profiles. Mullions and transoms are often not of the same depth, for structural reasons, but can be made so if required to support blinds, for example, or for visual reasons.

Where framing members have long vertical or horizontal spans, mild steel sections are sometimes used instead of a rectangular box section in aluminium, particularly if the equivalent aluminium section would be visually too deep or if the glazing system is fixed back to a steel frame forming part of the primary structure. The front part of the extrusion containing the seals is fixed directly to a mild steel box or T-section. The glazing is then fixed to this extrusion in the conventional way. If the steel frame has variable or complex curves then the rubber-based seals are set onto the steel frame without an extrusion with a technique commonly used in glazed roof structures. The glass is fixed with pressure plates directly to the steelwork with a rubber-based profile set between the glass and supporting steel.

Opening lights

Windows, doors and smoke vents are fixed into stick glazing as items with their own frame rather than using the curtain wall framing directly. This is because the opening light usually needs its own drainage and weatherproofing profiles and seals. This gives the appearance of a thicker frame around opening lights than around the adjacent fixed lights. Drips and seals form a part of the secondary frame in the same way as if the light were glazed into any other form of construction such as an opening in a masonry

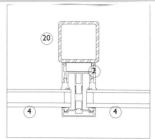

University Library, Delft, Holland. Architect: Mecanoo architekten bv.

Plans 1:10.

Plans 1:10. External corners

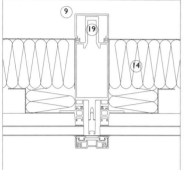

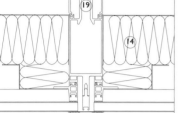

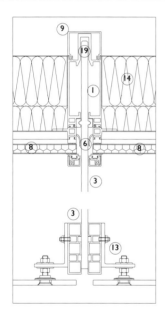

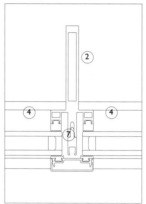

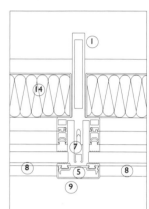

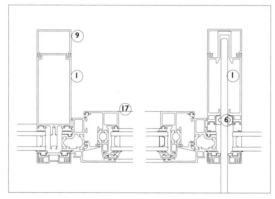

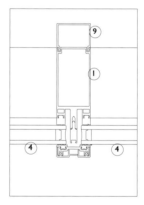

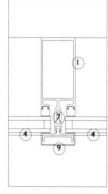

wall. The opening light is glazed into curtain walling around its edge with a thinner frame that corresponds to the thickness of the glazed units, allowing it to be fixed in place with the same technique as if it were a double glazed unit. These edge nibs are positioned on the frame to the opening light in a way that ensures that the glass of the opening light is in the same plane as the adjacent glass.

Parapets, cills and penetrations

Parapet copings are glazed into the curtain walling with a pressure plate in the same way as adjacent glazing. Copings usually project to align with the face of the cappings on the pressure plates or slightly forward of

them to protect the glazing beneath from the vertical movement of maintenance cradles. Copings slope inwards towards a gutter rather than sloping forwards to avoid dirt accumulating on the top of coping being washed down the facade by rain. This also avoids the need for the coping to project beyond the face of the glazing and form a drip. It should be noted that projecting drips on copings are still good practice in masonry construction, where an impervious coping washes rainwater onto a permeable masonry material beneath, causing staining. Cills at the base of stick glazing are formed with a pressed aluminium profile with a clip at the bottom which provides a clean line at the bottom of the wall, and provides rigidity to

the profile. Where cill drips can be seen from below, the folded edge provides a smooth painted edge which is also protected from weather corrosion.

Where stick glazing abuts an adjacent area of wall in a different material, a blocking profile is glazed into the edge of the glazing profile, faced with an EPDM foil. The foil is then bonded to the adjacent wall. Where glazing abuts metal rainscreens, which is a common combination, the edge of the metal return to the rainscreen can also be glazed into the edge mullion or transom. Where a projecting cill is required at the base of the wall, for example, a projecting aluminium cill is glazed into the curtain walling at the top

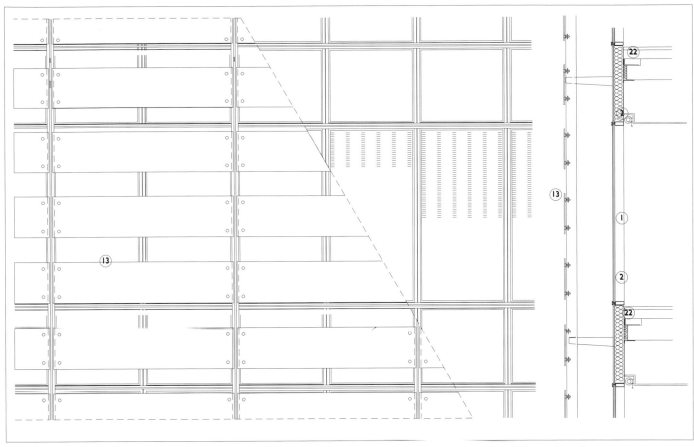

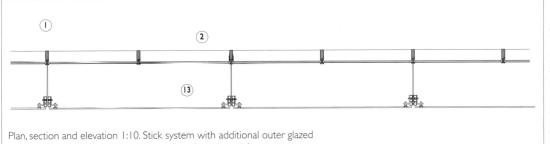

Plan, section and elevation 1:10. Stick system with additional outer glazed screen to provide solar shading or as part of a twin wall facade.

Details

1. Extruded aluminium transom
2. Extruded aluminium mullion
3. Fixing bracket
4. Single glazed or double glazed unit to suit application
5. Pressure plate
6. Rubber-based seal
7. Thermal break
8. Metal-faced or opaque glass-faced insulated panel
9. Cover cap
10. Floor slab
11. Floor finish
12. Ceiling finish
13. Outer glazed screen providing solar shading
14. Thermal insulation
15. Metal sheet seal
16. Maintenance access deck
17. Window glazed in curtain walling
18. Metal honeycomb panel
19. Slot in mullion to receive fixing bracket for external screens, etc.
20. Steel hollow section wall
21. Adjacent metal rainscreen shown
22. Smoke seal

end, and projects down over the adjacent wall in a manner to suit the detailing of the wall beneath.

Corners

Both internal and external corners are formed by glazing in a folded aluminium strip into the mullion on each side of the corner. Alternatively, a mullion set at 45° is used to give a thin edge to the facade, with a joint width similar to that of joints elsewhere on the facade. Some manufacturers provide interlocking mullions for use at corners to allow varying angles at corners on a single building with a constant abutting of mullions on the inside face.

Spandrel panels

Spandrel panels are made either as a continuous sealed panel, draining in the same way as the glass panels, or as a ventilated box. Where metal is used, spandrels can be formed as trays glazed into the framing with insulation between. Glazed spandrels are made either with rigid insulation bonded to the back of laminated glass or on a sheet of laminated glass with a ventilated void behind both to cool the glass and avoid either a visual read-through of the insulation from the outside or risk of the insulation delaminating from the glass. When glass is used it is made opaque (with either method) by screen printing, etching or a combination of both.

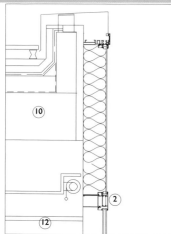

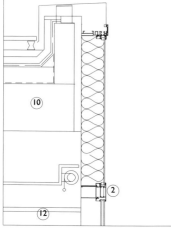

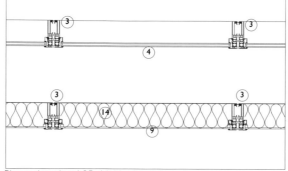

Plan and section 1:25. Unitised curtain walling

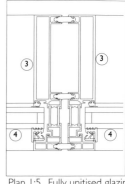

Plan 1:5. Fully unitised glazing

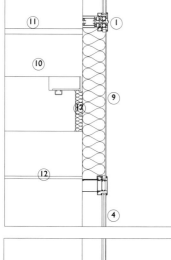

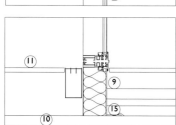

Details

1. Interlocking transom
2. Plain transom
3. Interlocking mullion
4. Single glazed or double glazed unit to suit application
5. Pressure plate
6. Rubber-based seal
7. Thermal break
8. Metal parapet coping
9. Metal-faced or opaque glass-faced insulated panels
10. Floor slab
11. Floor finish
12. Ceiling finish
13. Outer screen providing solar shading
14. Thermal insulation
15. Sheet metal seal
16. Cover cap
17. Smoke seal
18. Support bracket

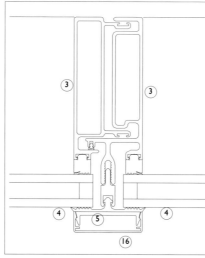

Plan 1:5. Semi-unitised glazing

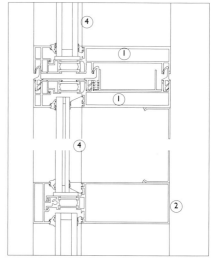

Plan 1:5. Fully unitised glazing

The main advantages of unitised glazing in construction are of speed of installation on site and of quality control of assembly workshop conditions over those on site. For taller buildings, for those over 5 or 6 storeys, scaffolding becomes much less practical, and so working from inside the building on a floor slab is a safer and faster method. Unitised panels are assembled and glazed in the factory. On site they are secured by brackets fixed to the floor slab and set side by side, then rising floor by floor, usually from the bottom of the building upwards. Panels are made either as panels set side by side, so that they can be replaced as complete panels if accidentally damaged, or be semi-interlocking where the glass is replaced without moving the panel.

The fully unitised type has wider site lines (overall frame width) at around 80mm (3in), than the semi-interlocking type at around 65mm (2.5in). A comparable stick system would have a joint width of around 50mm 2in). From the visual point of view, the wider site lines of unitised glazing over stick glazing is the main disadvantage of this system.

Unitised glazing is much less suited to tall glazed walls, visually, that have heights greater than around four metres between floor slabs, that is, greater than a single panel height. The framing can appear to be visually very strong, and instead frameless construction is often preferred as either bolt fixed or clamped glazing. Its most common use is in

modules of 1200mm or 1500mm wide (4ft or 5ft) where it suits the internal planning of office buildings, but storey height panels 3 metres wide are used. Because of the cost of setting up jigs and tools in the factory, unitised glazing is suited to use with a small number of panel types to create a high level of repetition. This suits very modular facades with relatively few panel types. Glazed units are fixed either with pressure plates, or are silicone-bonded to a light frame around the edge and then mechanically fixed to the frame of the panel.

Glazing

Glazed units are fitted either externally or internally depending on the glass replace-

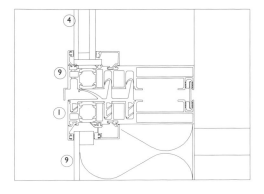

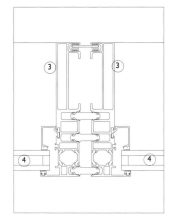

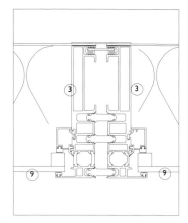

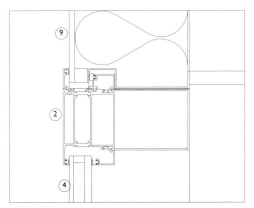

Sections 1:5. Junction with slab edge and parapet. System used in temperate climates.

RWE AG Essen, Germany. Architect: Ingenhoven Overdiek & Partner.

Elevation 1:50. Outer sealed glazed screen with inner sliding doors.

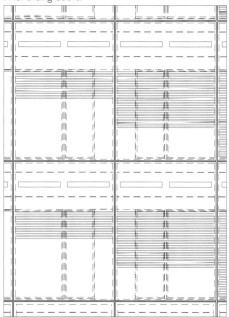

ment method. When glazed externally, mullions and transoms are adapted to have a clip on the outside to form a pressure plate. Where glazed units are internally glazed, clips are used which project from the sides of the mullion/transom section. This results in internally glazed sections usually being wider than those glazed externally. When glazed externally, a maintenance cradle is used with the capacity to lift glass and allow the panel to be lifted in place. This method allows glass to be replaced where it is either impractical to carry the glass through the building or where glass sizes are too large to enter stairwells or lifts. When internally glazed, glass units are carried up either in a lift or by stairs and are installed entirely from the floor

plate.

Jointing panels

Most panels are made one storey-height, but larger panels are made that span two floors and one bay wide or one storey high and several bays wide. Those larger panels are usually done where installation time is critical. Like stick glazing, panels are either hung from the top or are supported at the bottom. Instead of a straightforward spigot between storey height lengths of mullion, panels are tied together with a 'stack' joint, so-named from the concept of panels being stacked above one another. The complete bottom horizontal edge of the panel intersects with the top edge of the panel below.

This joint comprises two lines of defence against air and water infiltration, and a further air seal at the interior face of the panels. In stick glazing, seals are provided by a set of pressure plates applied when the carrier frame and glass are already in place. In unitised glazing, the waterproofing is mostly fixed to the panel before installation and has to work when panels are simply slotted into place. An outer line of defence is provided by rubber-based baffles set on each panel so that they press together to form a seal. An aluminium drip profile is sometimes added to the outside of this as a first barrier against wind, but allowing water to drip out again behind this profile. Any water passing through this profile is stopped in a pressure

Section 1:5. External sun shading glass fin shown.

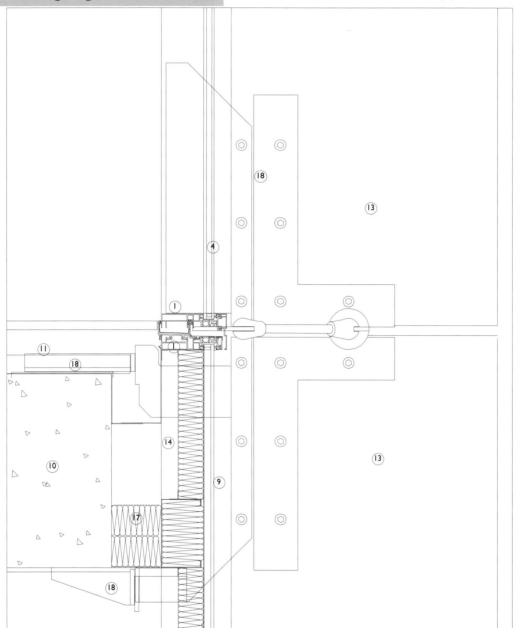

Details
1. Interlocking transom
2. Plain transom
3. Interlocking mullion
4. Single glazed or double glazed unit to suit application
5. Pressure plate
6. Rubber-based seal
7. Thermal break
8. Metal parapet coping
9. Metal-faced or opaque glass-faced insulated panels
10. Floor slab
11. Floor finish
12. Ceiling finish
13. Outer screen providing solar shading
14. Thermal insulation
15. Sheet metal seal
16. Cover cap
17. Smoke seal
18. Support bracket

As the size of the corner panel increases, it becomes more difficult to lift and set in place, and consequently becomes more expensive. A corner unit with a framing member at the corner can be made either with a frame visible, or visible only from the inside, with a glass-to-glass junction as described in the paragraph. Sometimes the joint occurs on the corner of two flat panels, with either a mitred corner or a square corner with an infill piece.

Both parapets and cills are formed in a similar way to those used on stick systems, but are formed as separate panels unlike stick systems which are glazed into the top transom at roof level.

Penetrations

Penetrations through glazing for brackets, usually fixed at floor level to fix them back to the floor slab, occur at joints between panels, through mullions or transoms. This is because the bracket can be far more easily sealed at this point, where the glazing system is drained and ventilated internally, than through spandrel panels, where it is difficult to apply a seal and where no mechanical pressure can be applied to the spandrel panel since there is no framing member behind.

Silicone-bonded glazing

A development over the past 10 years has been in silicone-bonded glazing. Although this is used in unitised systems, it is also used

partially in stick glazing. The glass is restrained on two vertical sides by pressure plates and two horizontal sides by silicone. Alternatively, the glass is bonded on all four sides by silicone. This method avoids the need for visible cappings for mullions and/or transoms which are often around 1.5 times wider than an equivalent stick system. The use of silicone allows the joint between glass units to be flush rather than using a pressure plate which is set in front of the glass. This allows the facade to have no visible framing on the outside. Silicone is also used in the joint since this material cannot be combined with an EPDM, such as neoprene, used in seals in pressure plate systems.

RWE AG Essen, Germany. Architect: Ingenhoven Overdiek & Partner.

Section 1:10. External sun shading metal panel shown.

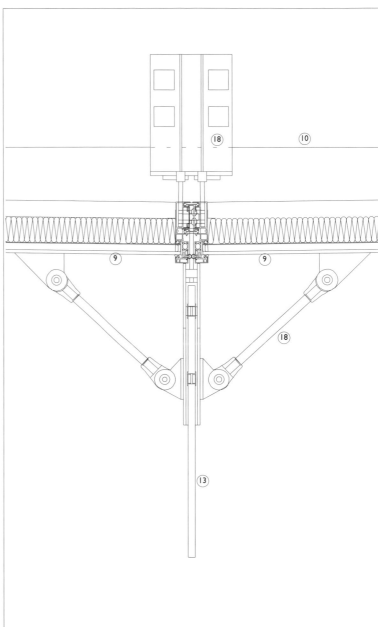

The glass units are bonded to aluminium profiles to form a light frame at the edge of the glass. The glass is then mechanically fixed with screws to the carrier frame on site. This technique is increasingly used in unitised systems where damaged glass can be removed without the need to remove the complete panel. Although silicone-bonded glazing allows a facade to appear from the outside as a continuous glass surface interrupted only by smooth and narrow joints, with 20mm (0.78in) rather than 50mm (2in) minimum with pressure plates, the opaque zone across the frame is the same overall width as with pressure plates. This is because the area behind the double glazed units is made opaque with screen printing in order to conceal the width of the carrier frame behind.

Some manufacturers bond a light aluminium frame around the edge of the frame within the depth of the double glazed unit, fixing the glass with short lengths of pressure plate in the conventional manner, then applying sealant into the joint. Sometimes the glass is secured by additional short clips along the horizontal edges to increase the safety of the system, but building codes around the world differ in this requirement.

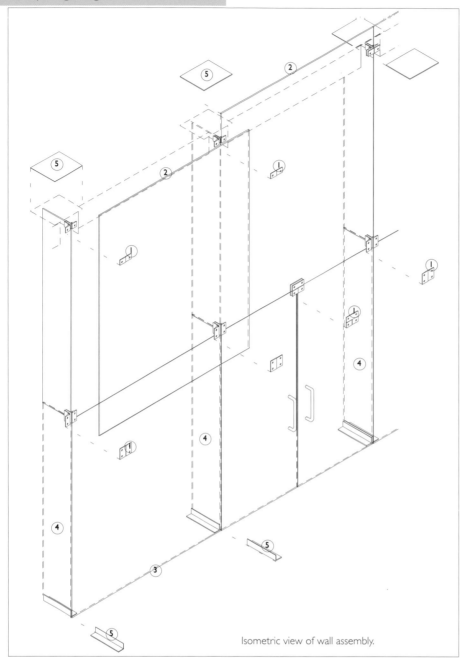

Isometric view of wall assembly.

Mediatheque, Sendai, Japan. Architect: Toyo Ito & Associates.

This glazing method is suited primarily to single glazing but double glazed examples are being constructed that avoid some of the wide joints resulting from the visible black edges of double glazed units. The sealant between double glazed units is also usually black to match the unit edges.

Comparison with bolt fixed glazing

As a method of frameless glazing, clamped glazing is more economical than bolt fixed glazing. Where bolt fixed glazing requires drilling of glass, clamped glazing does not, as glass is fixed with patches or clamps that pass through the joint between the glass sheets or double glazed units. The ability of clamp brackets to be simple and easily made

allows the glass to be supported at different angles to one another, in a tiled, non-planar manner. Glass has been lapped in the manner of traditional patent glazing and tiled in the manner of wood shingles, where glass is lapped on two edges to give a rich, undulating texture across glass facades. Because the facade is more visually vibrant, the fittings themselves can also project from the facade to allow less expensive stainless steel angle-type brackets to be used. These contrast both in the appearance and higher costs associated with bolt fixed glazing. A disadvantage of clamped glazing is that glass thicknesses are usually thicker than those in bolt fixed glazing, where the distances between fixings are reduced (reducing the span of the

glass) by setting them into the material.

This combination of easily fabricated, easily modified brackets and fixing through the joint allows a geometrically complex facade to be fixed back to a rectilinear, economic supporting structure. This contrasts with the need to repeat expensive bolt fixings where there is little possibility of changing the geometry to allow for different fixing positions of the glass.

Clamped glazing is increasingly used in rainscreen configuration with open joints or open, lapped joints with an accessible area behind, as used in 'twin wall' glazed facades. The outer screen acts primarily as a weather

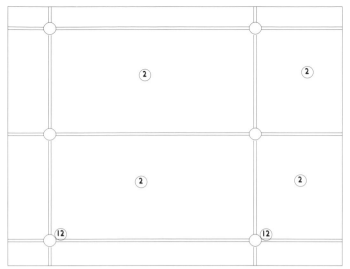

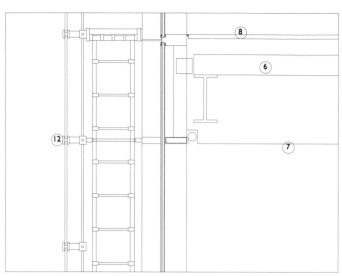

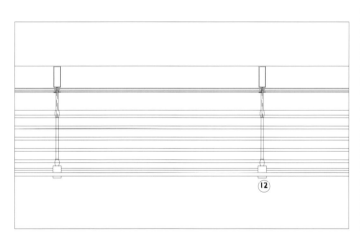
Plan, section and elevation 1:25. Twin wall construction with outer wall in clamped glazing..

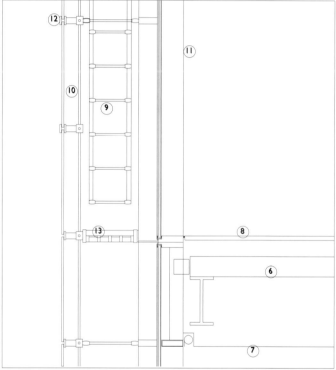

barrier, allowing the inner wall to have opening windows where they would otherwise not be possible, as in tall buildings or buildings in areas of high ambient noise. The rainscreen principle has been developed further to avoid fixing clamps directly to the glass but instead to silicone bond an edge frame around the glass and fix the frames back to supporting structure with clamps. This silicone-bonded variation of clamped glazing is very useful in opaque or translucent glazing in a full rainscreen to an opaque backing wall. Joints between the glass can be sealed with rubber-based strips to avoid dirt getting into the void behind the glass and staining the back of the glass. The advantage of this system is in clamping the glass by means of a

secondary frame that avoids penetrating an outer seal, thus making it suitable for glass rainscreen walls without visible framing and without the need for cleaning the inner face of the glass sheets.

Patch plate glazing

This method uses angles and plates that are bolted through the glass rather than through the joints. This is an earlier form of frameless glazing and was the forerunner of bolt fixed glazing. Although cheaper than bolt fixed glazing, it is restricted to single glazing. Glass sheets are fixed at their corners with a patch fitting that connects four sheets together. Like framed glazing in either stick or unitised systems, the glazing is either hung

from the top with either brackets or continuous stainless steel angles fixed back to the primary structure, or seated on support angles at its base. Patch fittings are not usually at top or base of a wall. Instead, continuous angles or a glazing channel is visually preferred both top and bottom in order to provide a weathertight seal. Clamped angles are used where they are concealed beneath floor finishes. Glazing channels are used either for convenience or where the channel is visible at floor level. Where glazed balustrades are used, these clamps are not sufficient for cantilevered glass, that is, where the glass is fixed only at floor level and not restrained at the level of the handrail. Doors are fixed using patch plates where the door

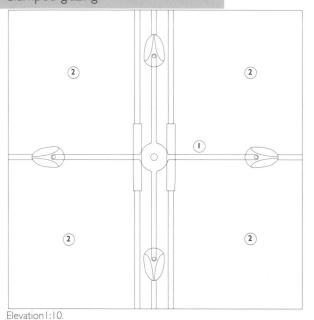

Elevation 1:10.

Section 1:10.

Plan, section and elevation 1:10. Clamped glazing with cast steel clamps held in place by forming part of a continuous truss.

Plan 1:10.

Isometric view of clamp assembly

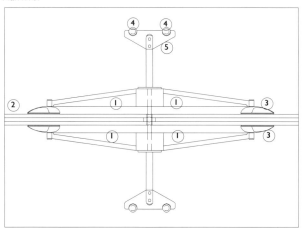

edges as it is easier to sit them in the shoes. Sometimes clips along vertical joints are used for lateral restraint but this depends very much on the specific design.

An alternative method of fixing the glass is to use a silicone-bonded frame around the glass and fixing that to cables or steel tubes. The joint between the glass is sealed with extruded silicone gaskets that can provide two lines of defence against windblown rain instead of the single line provided by site-applied silicone sealant. The use of extruded silicone allows the seal to be fixed to the unit in the factory, allowing the wall to be built in the manner of unitised glazing without the need for site scaffolding. Units are fixed from

mast climbers or from scaffolding.

Opaque glazing

This system comprises single glazing bonded back to aluminium frames which are clamped to a supporting structure, typically a concrete blockwork wall or hollow terra-cotta block. Clamps are fixed between joints from the front as short lengths of pressure plate. Alternatively, panels may be hooked onto rainscreen-type support brackets before being clamped in place. Unlike rain-screen construction, the joints between pan-els are sealed with an extruded profile or rubber-based seal onto which the glass is fixed. Parapets are partially ventilated to

avoid most of the water ingress but allow some ventilation. The bottom is also ventilat-ed, allowing moisture to find its way out. Opaque glazing can be easily integrated into adjacent areas of clear glazing by setting the aluminium extrusion away from the edge and fixing the edge of the glass into the adja-cent glazing system.

Sealing clamped glazing against adjacent construction

With all forms of clamped glazing, the movement or deflection of any fixed edges must be compatible with that of the general support system. This is particularly important in the case of cable-supported glazing, where

Plan, section and elevation 1:25. Clamped glazing with cast steel clamps held in place by forming part of a continuous truss.

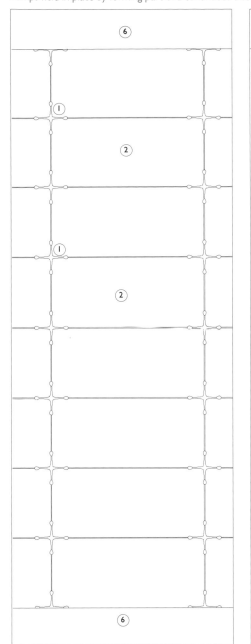

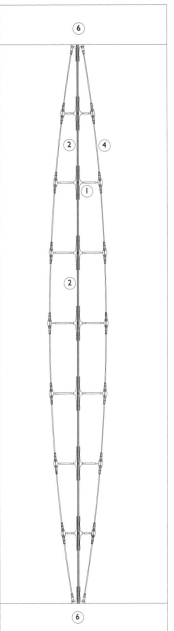

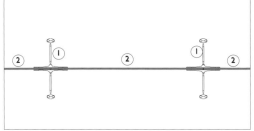

Details

1. Cast metal fixing bracket
2. Single glazed or double glazed unit to suit application
3. Cast or machined metal clamp
4. Stainless steel cable
5. Metal connector
6. Floor slab

Mediatheque, Sendai, Japan. Architect: Toyo Ito & Associates.

high deflections associated with the cables must be integrated with the small amounts of movement when the glass at the edge of the wall is fixed onto an adjacent form of construction such as a reinforced concrete wall. The edge channel or fixings must allow the glass to rotate within it to take up movement from deflection in a cable supporting the other end of the glass. Seals are usually formed by glazing channels or steel angles that provide a weathertight seal. High amounts of movement can be taken up at junctions with a flexible metal strip that is silicone-bonded to the edge of the glass to provide a flexible seal.

Elevation 1:50. Typical layout of panels where cantilevered support brackets are used

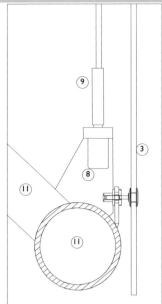

Elevation. Typical fixing arrangement for bolt fixed panels

Details

1. Cast steel connector
2. Mild steel or stainless steel angle bracket
3. Single glazed or double glazed unit to suit application
4. Outer silicone seal with inner rubber-based extruded seal
5. Insulated panel
6. Bolt-based cable end
7. Stainless steel bolt fixing
8. Steel connector fixed to steel tube
9. Stainless steel cable
10. Floor slab/structural wall
11. Glazing channel at floor level
12. Structural column. Concrete shown
13. Steel arm for lateral support
14. Steel rod

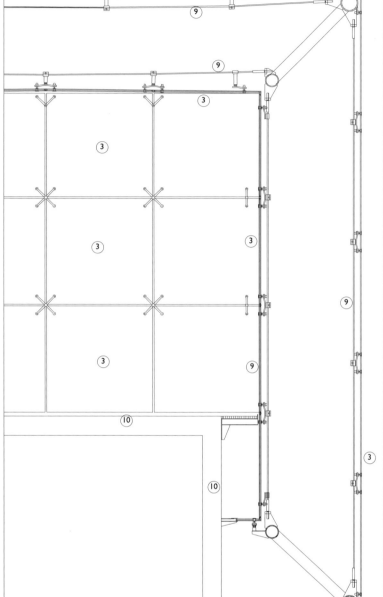

Hong Kong Railway Station. Architect: Ove Arup and Partners.

Like clamped glazing, bolt fixed glazing has a high degree of transparency provided by the bolts which replace the need for metal framing around the edges of the glass sheet or double glazed units. One of the main advantages of bolt fixed glazing is the small size of the fixings when compared to the larger and more frequent clamped fixings. This system can also be double glazed much more easily since a spacer can be introduced into double glazed units, during manufacture, away from the edge of the glass, where they also have the advantage of reducing the glass span, thus minimising glass thickness. However, the sight lines associated with double glazed units are almost the same as those for stick glazing, with the black line around the

edge of two adjacent units, plus a 20mm (0.78in) average joint in silicone giving an overall 50mm (2in) thick joint width in a dark colour. Since the edges of double glazed units are made opaque to conceal the edging strip, translucent silicone is not used in the joint between two opaque edges. Instead, a dark coloured silicone is used, usually black.

Support methods

In common with some other glazed wall types, bolt fixed glazing is either hung from the top of the unit or is supported at the bottom. When hung from the top, bolt fixings are secured to stainless steel cables or rods fixed at the top and tensioned at the

bottom. Fixing tolerances are provided in three directions: vertically, horizontally and laterally. Because the joints between the glass units or sheets are visible, and need to be well aligned, and the fact that the glass is drilled during the manufacture of the glass, fixing tolerances have to be provided by the bolt fixing and its connection to the supporting bracket.

The bolt fixings themselves vary in complexity from economic types where a threaded bolt is secured with nuts to a fixing bracket, to sophisticated types where all threads are concealed behind sleeves to give a very smooth appearance. All bolt types allow rotation to occur between the glass

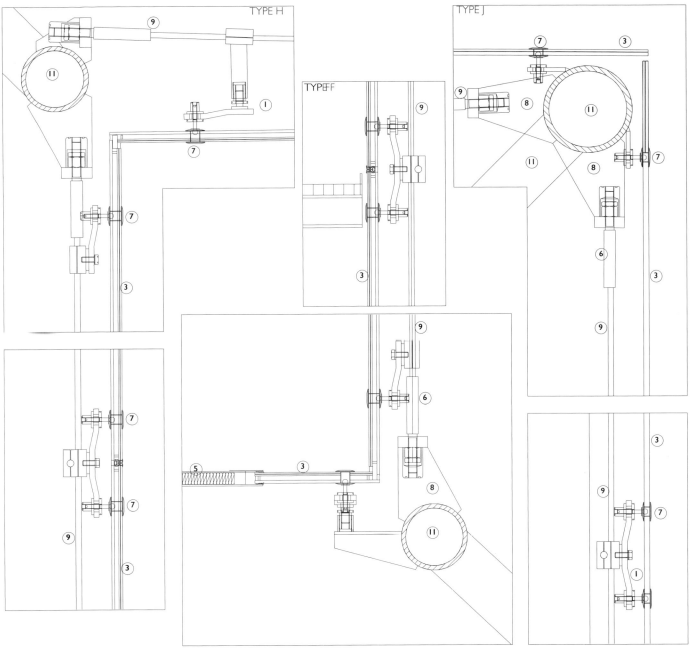

Sections 1:10. Bolt fixed walls and roof with additional bolt fixed outer wall in double wall configuration

TYPE H

TYPE J

TYPE FF

and the fixing usually to a maximum of 12 degrees. A ball joint is housed where the fixing intersects with the glass for this purpose. Any sleeve that is set over the threaded rod behind the disc is positioned so that it does not interfere with the free movement of the ball joint. Support brackets to bolts are either cast or are machined and welded from plate. The choice will depend largely on shape and the number of brackets needed, since castings are economic only in large numbers cast from a single mould. Castings can be formed to take up complex geometries that look very cumbersome in welded plate, but are more expensive and time-consuming to produce, except in large quantities. The choice of painted mild steel or

stainless steel (polished or brushed) for the support bracket is very much a visual decision, particularly where a large amount of welding is required. If the welding is not performed to the highest standards then the results can be visually disappointing. However, the bolts themselves are always in stainless steel. Junctions between mild steel and stainless steel are isolated to avoid the strong electrolytic corrosion that occurs between these two metals.

Construction tolerances between supporting structure and glass panels are accommodated between the glass and the bolt fixing, between the bolt fixing and the support bracket, or 'spider' and between the

support bracket and the supporting column or truss. The gap between glass bolt and fixing is to allow three of the typical four bolt fixings on a glass unit to move freely, while the fourth unit is clamped tight without damaging the glass at the edge of the hole. If adjustment is provided between bolt fixing and support bracket in order to take up dimensional differences between glass and supporting structure then this results in different joint widths between glass units, with slightly uneven corners where four glass units meet. This method does, however, allow the support spider to be set in a fixed relationship with the supporting truss or column. If this adjustment is instead formed between spider and primary structure, then

Town Hall and Theatre, Ijsselstein, Holland. Architect: UN studio van Berkel & Bos.

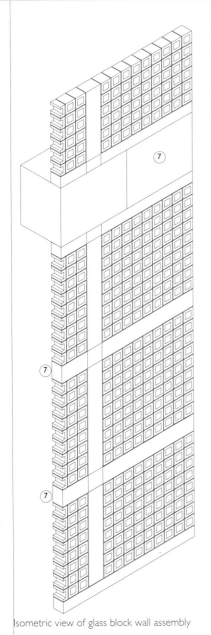

Glass channel details

1. Single skin of cast glass channels
2. Double skin of interlocking cast glass channels
3. Enclosing wall. Light gauge steel from wall shown
4. Extruded aluminium edge channel

Glass block details

1. Glass block
2. Bedding reinforcement
3. Bedding compound, mortar or silicone-based bond.
4. External cladding
5. Metal flashing
6. Thermal insulation
7. Enclosing wall or adjacent wall
8. Steel or reinforced concrete support frame

Isometric view of glass block wall assembly

Town Hall and Theatre, Ijsselstein, Holland. Architect: UN studio van Berkel & Bos.

eral stability through its height. Glass blocks are bonded together with silicone which allows for the higher amounts of structural movement associated with steel supports than those in reinforced concrete structures. The continuous surface of blocks, uninterrupted by floor slabs or concrete beams, do not require any drips to throw water clear of these surfaces, giving an overall smooth appearance to the glass block wall.

Masonry and timber framed window openings

Glass blocks cannot be bedded directly into masonry walls, such as concrete blocks, since any movement at joints between blocks will result in a crack in the nearest glass

blocks. For this reason when glass blocks are held in masonry openings, they can be set directly onto a concrete cill if one is used. Sometimes the concrete cill can form a complete reinforced concrete frame, around 50 -75mm (2in-3in) wide in which the glass blocks are set. Openings in timber framed walls, and openings in cavity wall construction (typically brick outer leaf, air gap and inner block/timber wall) use an extruded aluminium frame to hold the glass blocks in place, which is usually polyester powder coated. The aluminium frames are thermally broken, fixed to the masonry opening, usually with screws. Similar aluminium sections are used between some joints to provide additional support if required. Where glass blocks

are set into an opening in a timber frame, the aluminium profile edge can be combined with a timber cill to give a continuous timber appearance both internally and externally.

Cast glass channels

The effect of translucency provided by thick glass can also be provided by cast glass channels. These are like half blocks in section which are made in lengths up to around 2.5 metres (1ft 6in). Most are around 250mm wide × 60mm deep (10in × 2.5in) with glass around 6-7mm (0.25in) thick. Planks can be set both vertically and horizontally, but vertical applications are the most common as they are far easier to fix. When set horizontally, glass planks cannot sit on top of one

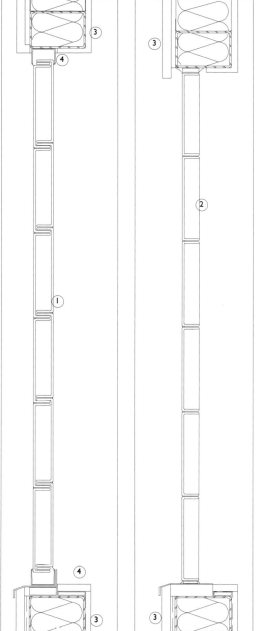

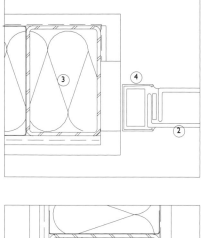

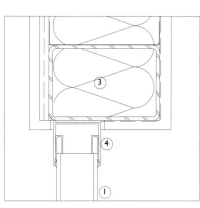

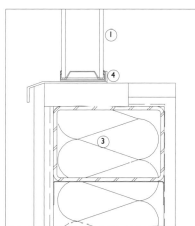

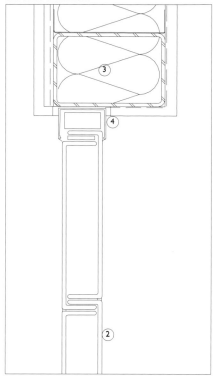

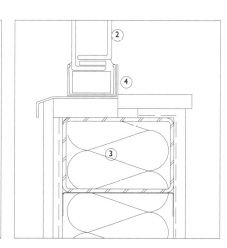

another; each plank is supported individually at its end to provide a waterproof seal between planks that can accommodate thermal movement.

An advantage of cast glass channels or 'planks' over glass blocks is that they are self-supporting, with the ability to span their full length of around 2.5 metres (8ft). The glass is held in place with thermally broken aluminium extrusions at its ends, using sections similar to those used for glass blocks in window openings. The extrusions are anodised or polyester powder coated to suit the design. Light transmission is around 85%, reducing to 70% if two channels are interlocked to form a wall of double thickness to improve thermal insulation and increased sound

reduction through the wall. A double thickness of interlocking channels can provide a sound reduction similar to that of a double glazed unit in a glazed wall of around 40dB, with thermal insulation also similar to that of a double glazed unit at around 2.0 W/m^{2}K if a hard low emissivity (low e) coating is applied to the inner face of the outer channel. An advantage of cast glass channel glazing is that it is much cheaper than a conventional glazed wall system. This coating changes the surface appearance slightly. A hard coating allows the channels to be assembled on site. The higher performance soft coatings are required to be sealed as double glazed units in the factory, which is not possible with cast glass channels as their

ends are open until installed in the aluminium edge framing already described.

Cast glass channels are sealed together with silicone, with translucent white being the most commonly used colour, to match the glass as closely as possible. Unlike glass blocks, cast glass channels can provide only very limited fire resistance of around 30 minutes when the length of the plank is restricted to around 2.5 metres (8ft). The glass is reinforced with a grid of wires, giving the appearance of traditional wired glass, and joints use a fire retardant silicone.

Plans and sections 1:5. Rolled steel frames with double glazed units

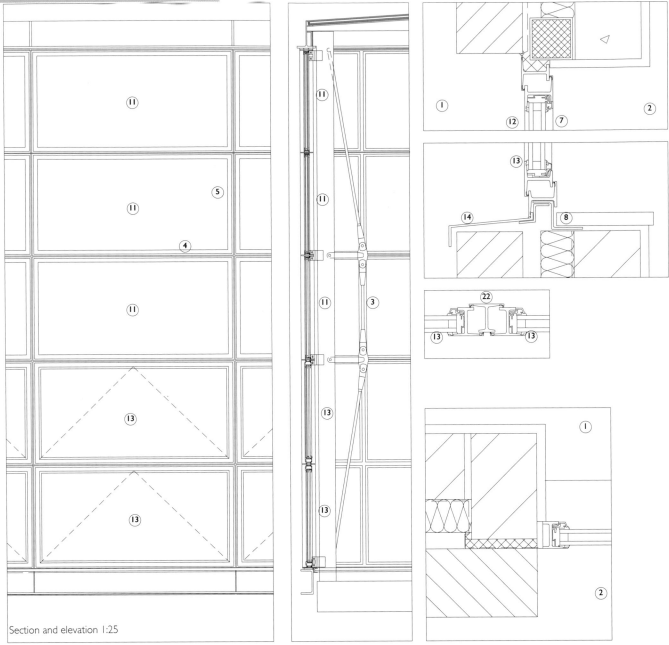

Section and elevation 1:25

Steel framed windows are a robust window construction that is often used as a fire resistant glazing. Steel glazing was developed primarily for single glazing, where the main advantage was their thin sight lines when compared to those in aluminium. The thin, rigid, rolled steel sections were also more economic than their aluminium counterparts. The rolled sections can accommodate double glazed units of most thicknesses, but are not thermally broken. These rolled sections are used with small window sizes up to a maximum of around 3000 × 1800mm (10ft × 6ft) and a minimum of 250mm × 400mm (10in × 16in) with double glazed units. Fully glazed walls made from window sections can be made using this relatively small window

size. The 'window wall' is stiffened with a frame formed from integral steel fins that pass through the window. These narrow window sections cannot incorporate a thermal break.

Window walls with larger panel sizes can be formed in larger pressed steel sections and rolled hollow sections rather than the smaller G-shaped or T-shaped sections. Their sight lines are very similar to those in aluminium, that is considerably wider than hot rolled sections. Pressed steel sections are wider and deeper in section than the rolled types but they have the advantage of being able to be formed into larger walls as well as being able to incorporate a thermal break.

Thermal breaks are held in place by folding the material tightly over the ends of the polymer material, which is currently too difficult to do economically in thin hot rolled sections.

The most common use of steel windows is in fire resistant glazing, typically where glazed walls enclose a fire resisting compartment. The fire integrity is usually between 30 minutes and 1 hour, but 2 hour integrity can be achieved when used with fire resisting glasses. Although steel glazing provides structural integrity during a fire, it does not provide thermal insulation to counter the heat generated by fire. This is dealt with either by providing sprinklers that drench the wall to

Sections 1:5. Rolled steel frames glazed internally and externally

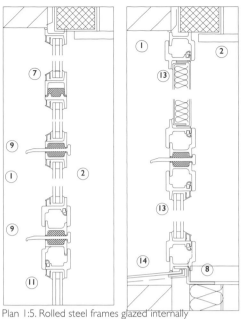

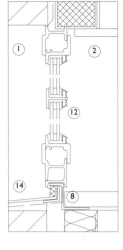

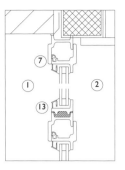

14. Window cill
15. Condensation tray
16. Damp proof course (DPC)
17. Internal finish
18. Drip
19. Packing
20. Aluminium clip to secure double glazed unit
21. Steel cill
22. Meeting stile

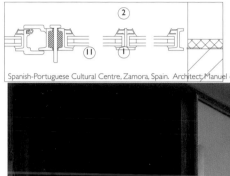

Plan 1:5. Rolled steel frames glazed internally

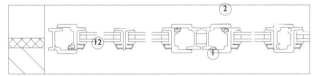

Plan 1:5. Rolled steel frames glazed externally

Spanish-Portuguese Cultural Centre, Zamora, Spain. Architect; Manuel de las Casas.

Details

1. Outside
2. Inside
3. Steel supporting structure
4. Transom
5. Mullion
6. Single glazed or double glazed unit to suit application
7. Fixing bead
8. Fixing lug
9. Projecting transom
10. Rubber-based seal
11. Fixed light
12. Inward opening light
13. Outward opening light

keep it cool or else the wall is positioned in a way that building users do not come into direct contact. Areas of fire resisting glazing can be combined with areas of unprotected glass without changing the outward appearance of the glazing. This is a big advantage where a consistency of appearance is required over a continuous facade with different requirements for fire protection in different areas of the same facade.

Small-scale glazing

Fixed and opening lights framed in sizes up to 3000mm x 1800mm (10ft x 6ft) use a standard single section which is used for both horizontal and vertical glazing sections as well as for opening lights. Where opening lights occur, the profile used for the window frame is different, as is the profile for the opening light itself. Also, profiles are different for inward and opening lights. Unlike aluminium framed glazed walling, where a single extrusion is used throughout, with opening lights glazed into the system, small-scale steel glazing requires a family of different profiles to create a single glazed wall. For this reason, manufacturers offer a small range of steel window types in order to remain economic. Because sections are rolled rather than extruded, there is very little possibility of creating a new profile for a specific project. Single glazed panes of glass were traditionally fixed with steel pins and glazing putty like traditional window frames, but the practice

has given way to thin steel channels and angles. More recently, aluminium extrusions are used, which are clipped into place. The extrusions are both more reliable in the long term and far easier to replace, particularly in large-scale glazed walls.

When windows, either fixed or opening lights, are joined together to form a glazed wall, mild steel T-section fins are set between the windows to form a stiffening frame. The adjacent frames are screwed to the fins in order to contribute to the overall stiffness of the frame. Unlike aluminium, the T-section used is different from those set vertically in order to provide a projecting drip. Profiles are designed so that they are glazed from

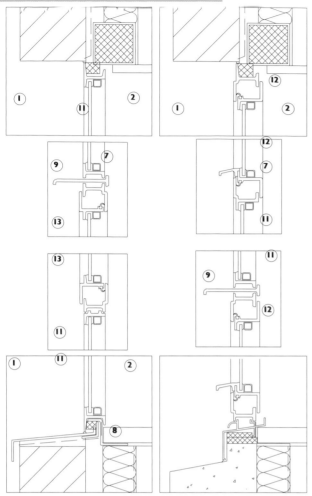

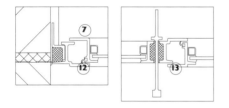

Sections 1:5. Rolled steel frames with single glazing

Details

1. Outside
2. Inside
3. Steel supporting structure
4. Transom
5. Mullion
6. Single glazed or double glazed unit to suit application
7. Fixing bead
8. Fixing lug
9. Projecting transom
10. Rubber-based seal
11. Fixed light
12. Inward opening light
13. Outward opening light
14. Window cill
15. Condensation tray
16. Damp proof course (DPC)
17. Internal finish
18. Drip
19. Packing
20. Aluminium clip to secure double glazed unit
21. Steel cill
22. Meeting stile

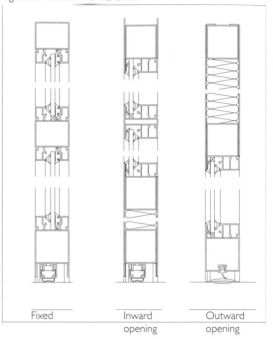

Sections 1:5. Pressed steel single glazed fire resisting doors without thermal breaks

| Fixed | Inward opening | Outward opening |

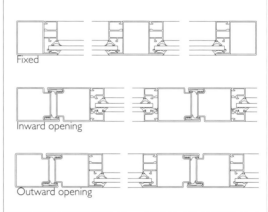

Fixed

Inward opening

Outward opening

Plans 1:5. Pressed steel single glazed fire resisting doors without thermal breaks

---

either the inside or the outside. The choice of system is usually dictated by the method of glass replacement, which may be from an internal floor or from an external ladder or cleaning and maintenance cradle.

Outward opening lights have profiles with edges that project over the front of the supporting frame to exclude rainwater. A projecting drip is provided at the top to protect the vulnerable top joint. Any rainwater that drips into the inner surface of the frame is drained away around the edge of the frame and out at the bottom of each frame. Rubber-based seals are now used to assist with reducing air infiltration through the window.

Inward opening lights use the same profiles with their projecting edges set against the frame in a similar way. At the window head, a projecting fin is not needed as a drip, since the outer frame is lapped over the inner light. Rubber-based seals are used to reduce air infiltration. Windows and glazed walls are fixed to adjacent masonry walls with steel lugs that allow them to be fixed away from the edge of the concrete or masonry. These lugs are concealed by internal finishes. When fixed into a timber or pressed steel edge frame, steel glazing can be fixed directly through the frame into the supporting material.

Additional stiffening for larger walls is

provided by tube or box sections set away from the glazed wall. The glazing is fixed to the support frame with steel cleats and brackets. These provide a method of taking up tolerances and alignment adjustments between the windows and their supporting frame.

Doors are fixed to the supporting frame in the same way as windows, but their construction is more robust. They have thicker sections at the cill and have a horizontal rail at mid-height to provide stiffness. Some also have mild steel plates, glazed in at cill level as kicking plates. The plates have an internal insulation core if used in conjunction with double glazing. The thinness of steel window

Spanish-Portuguese Cultural Centre, Zamora, Spain. Architect: Manuel de las Casas.

Plans and sections 1:5. Pressed steel doors without thermal breaks

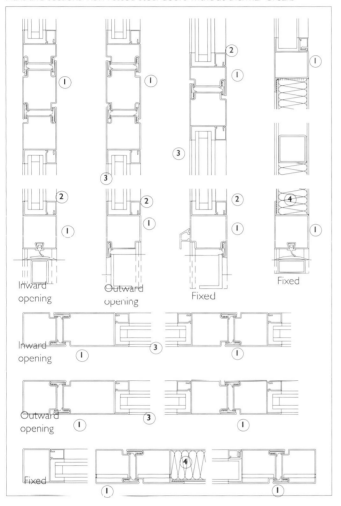

Sections 1:5. Pressed steel doors with thermal breaks

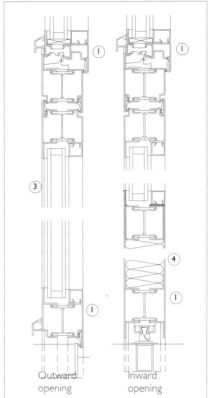

Steel framed doors and windows
1. Pressed steel frame
2. Pressed steel glazing bead
3. Double glazed unit
4. Insulated steel panel

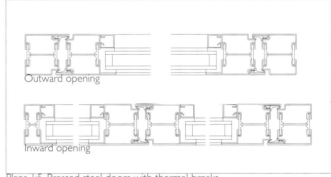

Plans 1:5. Pressed steel doors with thermal breaks

frames in relation to aluminium allow door cills to be visually more discrete than those in aluminium, with a low upstand formed by the cill at floor level. Doors, in common with other cills, have a condensation channel which collects water at the bottom of the glazed wall and directs it to the outside. These channels are needed since the frame is not thermally broken and condensation can occur on the internal face in temperate climates.

Large-scale glazing

Large-scale glazing uses a carrier frame of mullions and transoms formed in steel box sections similar to that in aluminium. The carrier frame has an indented groove at the

front to allow fixing toggles to be inserted into it. Rubber-based air seals are set against the carrier frame onto which the double glazed units are set. The glass is secured with pressure plates and integral rubber-based seals in the same way as aluminium glazed wall systems. The pressure plate is fixed with a bolt that is secured into the toggle. In aluminium construction, a projecting groove (1) forms part of the extrusion to which the bolt is fixed. Rolled or pressed steel cannot incorporate such a complicated and rigid profile. The rubber-based air seals fixed to the box sections have an additional lip which tucks down over the top of the double glazed unit below. This provides a sealed inner chamber for drainage and pressure

equalisation in the manner of aluminium glazed walls. Manufacturers provide systems to suit different glazing layouts and spans. The shape of the box section can also vary, from thin long boxes, to a rectangular box, to a pointed aerofoil-type section. The overall sight lines are thinner than an equivalent in aluminium. Special corner pieces are made within manufacturers' systems which are similar to those in aluminium. These special profiles make corners more elegant than they would be by combining structural sections, which would necessitate the adding of sheet metal in corners.

Parapets are formed by glazing a metal flashing into the transom (horizontal) at the

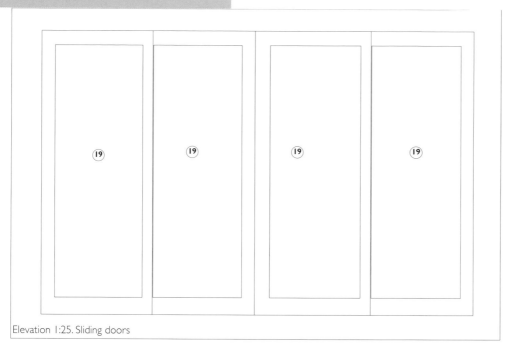

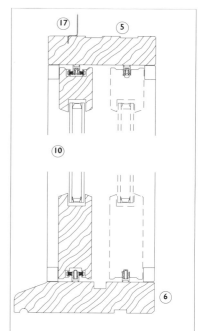

Elevation 1:25. Sliding doors

Details

1.	Fixed light	9.	Thermal insulation	16.	Internal finish
2.	Supporting structure	10.	Single glazed or double glazed unit to suit	17.	Flashing to seal against adjacent wall
3.	Outside		application	18.	Vertically sliding sash
4.	Inside	11.	Fixing bead	19.	Sliding door frame top hung or bottom
5.	Head	12.	Rubber-based seal		rolling
6.	Cill	13.	Inward opening light	20.	Sliding window or door jamb
7.	Metal stiffening insert	14.	Outward opening light		
8.	Timber infill panel	15.	Damp proof course (DPC)		

Plan and section 1:5. Sliding doors

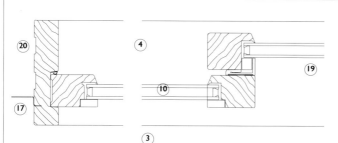
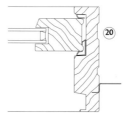
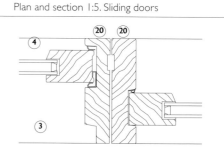

Windows in openings

Where timber windows are set into an opening rather than being part of a window wall, the most common materials used are masonry block, brick or timber boarding. With all these materials, timber windows are fixed either into the reveals of the opening or are fixed onto the face of the opening. The position of the window in the opening has more influence over the junction with the surrounding wall than the choice of material for the wall.

In (1), the window is fixed to the outside face of the wall, which would typically be reinforced concrete or concrete block. This would be used where a massive, sound insu-lating structure, such as an apartment build-ing, is clad in a different material such as tim-ber rainscreen panels or terracotta, which are often used in a smooth continuous plane without reveals. This construction is ideal for rainscreen construction. It allows the win-dow to be sealed to the structural wall, or backing wall, with a lapped joint around the opening and allowing it to be fitted indepen-dently of that opening. This permits the wall to be set out on a precise grid that would be difficult to achieve by setting the window into the opening. This is because the con-struction tolerances associated with con-crete frame construction are considerably higher than those used for timber windows. Windows would typically be sealed against the concrete wall with projecting profiles that would lap under a waterproof layer on the surrounding wall. This creates a deep reveal on the inside face of the wall which has finishes applied to create a tidy junction with the internal face of the window.

In (2), the window is set into the reveal of the opening. Because the window has to be smaller than the opening size in order to install it, the joint width has to be accurately formed around the window. Sometimes the window frame is built-in to the wall as the surrounding wall is constructed, or else a template is used to avoid accidental damage to the window during construction.

Elevation 1:25. Sliding doors

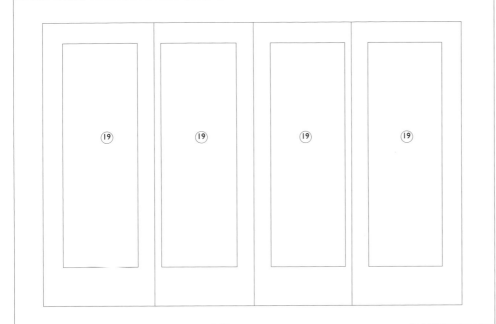

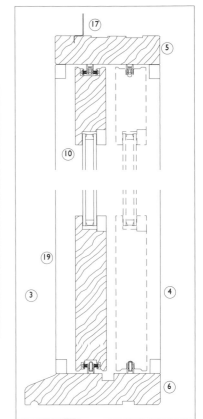

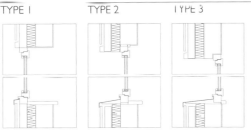

TYPE 1   TYPE 2   TYPE 3

Plan and section 1:5. Sliding doors

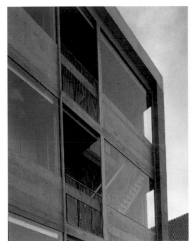

Housing, Tilburg, Holland.
Architect: (EEA) Erick van Egeraat associated architects

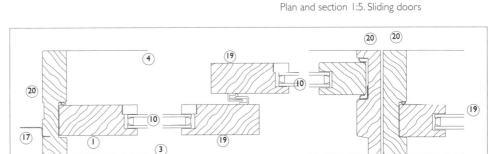

In (1) the window is set into the outer wall construction and needs to allow water to drain the top of the opening to the sides, as in masonry cavity wall construction. In (2) the window does not have this additional requirement, and so is protected from water penetration by the wall itself. However, rainwater needs to be drained at the bottom of the opening, where a cill is provided. The window is lapped over the cill, often with an additional weather bar for protection against water ingress through capillary action.

In (3) the window is set into a stepped reveal. This has the advantage of giving greater construction tolerance when fitting the window as well as creating a lapped joint between the structural opening and the window, which is easier to seal than an equivalent butt joint, where a backing strip is needed to give a surface to which the sealant can adhere.

Housing, Tilburg, Holland.
Architect: (EEA) Erick van Egeraat associated architects

3

CONCRETE

(1) **Cast in situ /**
   cast-in-place:
   Parapets, drips and cills
   Finishes
   As-cast finish
   Washed finish
   Polished finish

(2) **Storey height**
   precast panels:
   Panel types
   Thermal Insulation
   Joints
   Acid etched finish

(3) **Small precast cladding**
   panels:
   Individually supported
   panels
   Self supporting
   stacked panels
   Parapets and cills
   Openings
   Sand blasted finish
   and tooled finish

Concrete 03
In-situ loadbearing concrete walls

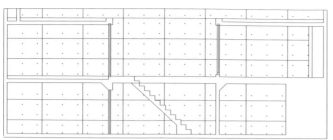

Internal wall elevation 1:50. Typical in situ cast concrete wall showing recessed joints erected by arrangement of formwork.

Setting reinforcement

Setting up formwork

Details

1. Concrete external wall
2. Concrete internal wall
3. Thermal insulation
4. Window frame
5. Waterproof membrane
6. Metal parapet flashing
7. Internal finish
8. Metal cill
9. Drip
10. Metal lined gutter

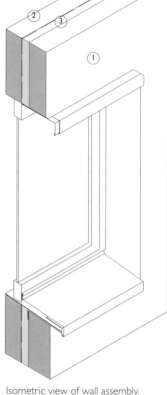

Isometric view of wall assembly.

CAC Museum, Cincinatti, USA. Architect: Zaha Hadid.

An essential difference between concrete and other materials used in facade construction is that concrete is poured in place into moulds, or into formwork, rather than being manufactured as a standard size component in a factory. Where metal, glass, masonry, plastics and timber are made to standard dimensions in the form of sheets or sections, concrete is cast, either on site or in a factory as precast panels. Although there are few constraints on the size of a single cast element in concrete, in practice an essential determinant of concrete panel size is the amount of concrete that can be poured at one time. With precast concrete the essential constraint on panel size is the weight that can be lifted by a crane on site.

In-situ concrete is dependent on the formwork in which the concrete is cast. An understanding of formwork is important to appreciate how to control the appearance of joints and of bolt holes through the concrete, since the formwork is the negative impression, or mirror image, of the final concrete.

The design of in-situ concrete walls has changed in recent years to include thermal insulation, either set within the concrete during pouring, or fixed on the internal face or external face after the wall has been cast. The position of the insulation within the construction affects the use of the thermal mass of concrete and its ability to contribute

to night-time cooling as part of an overall reinforced concrete structure. Continuity of thermal insulation is increasingly important in the interface with glazed openings and doors to avoid thermal bridging. Continuity of double glazing and thermal insulation in the concrete wall is probably the biggest recent change in this form of construction in recent years. In-situ concrete walls are formed as either a structural concrete wall with thermal insulation on the inside face with an internal dry lining, or as a diaphragm/double wall of concrete with thermal insulation set between the two skins of concrete.

The first method has the benefit of economy, particularly where the thermal

Setting up formwork

Setting up plywood formwork

Section and elevation 1:10.
Head and cill of window opening

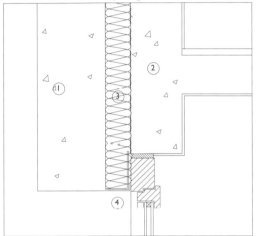

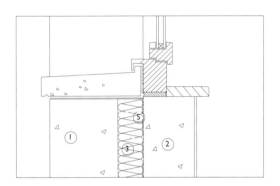

Section and elevation 1:50. In situ cast concrete wall cast in 2 skins with rigid closed cell insulation between skins

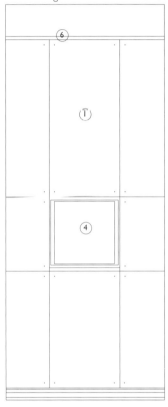

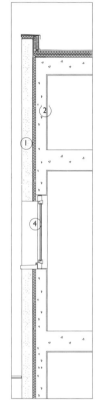

mass of the concrete wall is not required for use in night-time cooling. The wall zone for the insulation can also be used to fit windows, so that the opening lights and doors do not have to be set into specially cast recesses in the concrete, which makes it more expensive. Drips are cast into the tops of window reveals to reduce staining to the adjacent wall beneath caused by rainwater runoff from dust that accumulates on flat surfaces. Parapets have metal copings that prevent staining on the wall beneath by directing rainwater towards a gutter immediately behind the parapet.

With the second method, in-situ concrete walls are formed as 'sandwich' walls with internal insulation. These have either insulation broken by strips of concrete that link across the two skins (forming limited thermal bridges) or are formed as two separate concrete skins linked only by stainless steel brackets and ties. The second type is increasingly popular as it avoids thermal bridging with its associated risk of condensation forming on the inside of the wall, in temperate climates.

Parapets, drips and cills

The detailing of openings, parapets and cills follows the same principles for a single wall of structural concrete with internal thermal insulation. When concrete is used as an exposed external finish, cills, parapets and drips are detailed to ensure that rainwater is thrown as clear as possible from the external wall surface. When an additional outer material is used, typically a rainscreen in a wide range of materials, the concrete wall can be formed economically with no regard for visual appearance, since the material is not visible.

Since horizontal or slightly sloping surfaces catch dust, roof overhangs and deep eaves are often incorporated into the design to avoid wash-off from rain. Dust washed away by rainwater causes the deposit of dirt and dust in adjacent areas of wall. If overhangs are not a part of the design, then water from horizontal or slightly sloping sur-

Concrete 03
In-situ loadbearing concrete walls

Securing formwork

Concrete poured

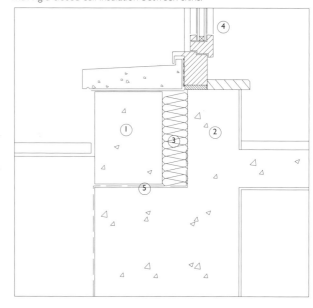

Details

1. Concrete external wall
2. Concrete internal wall
3. Thermal insulation
4. Window frame
5. Waterproof membrane
6. Metal parapet flashing
7. Internal finish
8. Metal cill
9. Drip
10. Metal lined gutter

Section 1:10. Junction at ground level for typical wall condition and for window/door condition. In situ cast concrete wall cast in 2 skins with rigid closed cell insulation between skins.

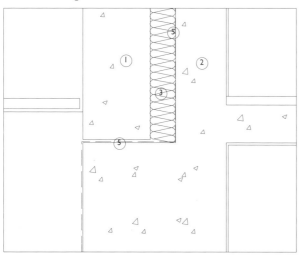

faces is thrown clear of the wall by projecting cills and flashings. In highly polluted environments, dust-catching wall textures are usually avoided, and smooth finishes are often preferred. However, where protective treatments are applied to the concrete to reduce porosity, this can lead to greater run-off across the facade which can increase staining, and must be taken into account in the design of the external wall.

Finishes

The main influence in the base colour of concrete used for wall construction is in the choice of cement, with fair-faced visible concrete walls using either a grey cement base or a white cement base. The physical proper-

ties of these two cement types is very similar.

The colour of finished concrete from a grey cement base is also grey, as expected, but this can vary with the water/cement ratio, the porosity of the shuttering, vibration conditions, formwork stripping time and weather conditions. The grey type can also blacken with rain due to the presence of iron oxide. However, grey cement based architectural quality concrete can achieve an even colour when pouring methods and conditions are kept consistent. When grey cement is used with a moderate to high level of pigment content, as-cast or treated concretes are much less prone to colour

variations due to the strong covering capacity of the pigments. White cement is much more expensive than grey cement but it is not subject to the colour variations of grey cement, nor is it subject to rain darkening.

The most common finishes used for in-situ cast concretes are an as-cast finish, a washed finish and a polished finish. The less common types are described in the following sections on precast panels, but can also be used for in-situ cast concrete walls, depending on the ability to work on large areas of completed wall surface.

As-cast finish

Smooth concrete finishes can have their

Concrete curing

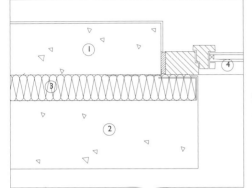

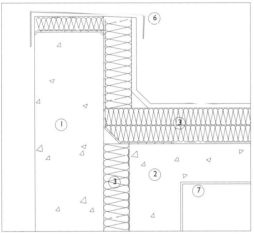

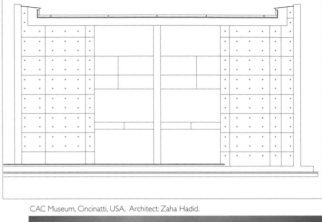

CAC Museum, Cincinatti, USA. Architect: Zaha Hadid.

Plan and section 1:10. Junction at parapet level for typical wall condition and for window jamb In situ cast concrete wall cast in 2 skins with rigid closed cell insulation between skins.

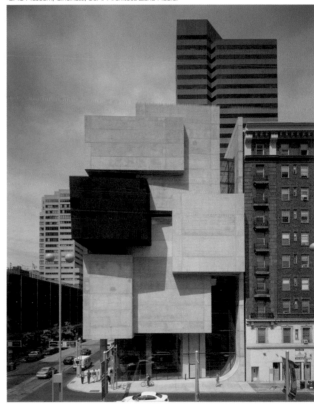

surfaces broken by small air bubbles of entrained air, but these hardly affect the surface any more than would be found in natural sandstones and limestones. Colour variations from the use of grey cement result not from its natural colour, but its colour after pouring, and from fine particles of sand becoming segregated in certain areas as a result of vibration. If these fine particles appear in the face of the wall, a marbling effect similar to that of natural stone will occur. If the particles are different from the shade of the facing, staining will occur. As a result, the tinting of clear mixtures with fine particles of dark sand is avoided. Smooth concrete is usually self-coloured, at least in large areas, to avoid colour variations associ-

ated with using pigment additives. Smooth and visually consistent natural finishes are achieved largely by both the accuracy of the proportions of the materials in the concrete mix, including water, and the care in preparing and setting the formwork.

Textured surfaces with either a shallow or deeper contoured profile can be formed either with specially fabricated shuttering boards or with an additional lining that is set on the inside face of the shuttering boards, against which the concrete is poured. An additional lining is usually flexible and is made of either polystyrene board, which can be used only once, or polyurethane sheet or silicone rubber sheet which can be used sev-

eral times. Silicone rubber moulds are made by pouring the material into a positive-shaped mould made from a non-cohesive material such as sand, making its use expensive, but capable of forming complex forms in the surface of as-cast concrete. Joints between these specially-made shuttering boards are usually formed as grooves to avoid uneven and blurred lines resulting from attempting to bond their edges.

Washed finish

The washing-out or deactivation of fresh concrete is carried out in two ways, either with 'faces shuttered' or with 'faces not shuttered'. The faces shuttered method involves the application of a product on the

Concrete 03
In-situ loadbearing concrete walls

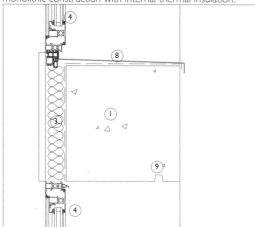

Concrete curing

Concrete curing

Removing formwork

Section 1:10.
Junction at window. In situ cast concrete wall cast as a monolithic construction with internal thermal insulation.

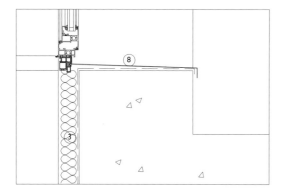

Details
1. Concrete external wall
2. Concrete internal wall
3. Thermal insulation
4. Window frame
5. Waterproof membrane
6. Metal parapet flashing
7. Internal finish
8. Metal cill
9. Drip
10. Metal lined gutter

CAC Museum, Cincinatti, USA. Architect: Zaha Hadid.

shutter panels that deactivates, retards or eliminates hydration of the cement. The product is applied with either a brush or by spraying. After stripping the shuttering, the external faces are washed with a water jet which removes the hydrated skin and, depending on how deep the effect of the deactivator is, reveals either the grains of sand or, more commonly, the coarse aggregate.

The faces not shuttered method is done either by spraying deactivator on the green (fresh) concrete and washing it as just described, or by direct washing before the cement has fully set. Usually the method is completed with a last wash using an aqueous

acid solution in order to remove traces of hydrated cement soiling the exposed aggregate, leaving stains on the outside face. When this is completed, the mineralogical nature of the coarse aggregate is exposed, which gives a textured appearance. Some aggregates, such as limestone, can become dulled or change colour on contact with the acid. In deep washing, this method is particularly suitable for bringing out the visual characteristics of coarse aggregate. It leads to a very different finish depending on the shape, either crushed or rolled, the mineralogical type (silica or limestone), particle size, but also the mix composition in terms of the density of stones revealed on the surface.

Polished finish

Concrete walls can be polished to varying amounts of smoothness by abrasive grinding, using a grinding wheel which is lubricated by water. The outer skin of the concrete is removed by abrasion to a depth of between 1mm and 2mm, with one pass of a grinding wheel which exposes some of the fine and coarse aggregate behind the surface. A second pass with a finer abrasion disc removes the big scratches left by the first pass, which are particularly visible on darker surfaces. With polishing by disc, a filler is applied to the surface to fill the air bubble pockets and small honeycombing. After this filler has hardened, the surface is again polished with successively finer grains. As the

Moving formwork to next floor up

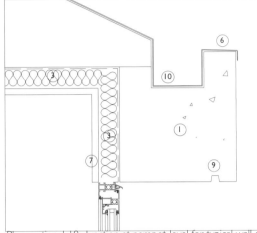
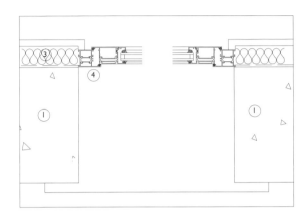

Plan, section 1:10. Junction at parapet level for typical wall condition and for window jamb. In situ cast concrete wall cast as a monolithic construction with internal thermal insulation.

Elevation 1:50. Typical in situ cast concrete wall

scratches are removed, the colours of aggregate reveal themselves, but the surface does not shine naturally. The concrete wall surface can, however, be made shiny by the application of a varnish. Concrete walls can be polished further to create a satin finish and even further to provide a gloss finish. A protective clear coating can also be applied at this point.

Polishing is easier to apply on flat surfaces than on roughened or curved areas of concrete. Polishing exposes the colour of the minerals within the concrete, giving rich colour effects from the cement, the sand, and the coarse aggregate materials in the mix. This method provides a self-coloured

finish with a surface which is less prone to retain dust, which washes off, causing staining, and is easy to maintain by simple washing, undertaken using the same methods of maintenance access used for glazed walls.

Next floor ready for new concrete

Isometric view of wall assembly.

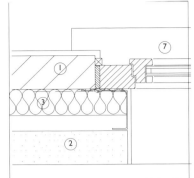

Plan 1:10.
Panel-to-panel junction and window jamb.

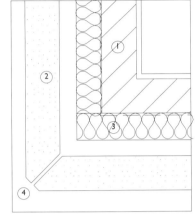

Plan 1:10. Panel junctions at corners.

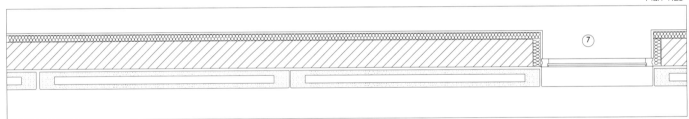

Plan 1:25

Smaller precast panels than those used in storey height sizes have been undergoing considerable development over the past 20 years. They are made as either individually supported panels or as self-supporting stacked panels.

Individually supported panels are fixed directly to a background supporting wall, usually formed either in reinforced concrete or in concrete block. Panels are usually open jointed to allow them to dry easily after wetting in rain and to allow rainwater to drain easily down the backs of the panels or down the face of the backing wall. Spandrel panels are usually part of a proprietary precast concrete system of frame, floor slab and spandrel panel, with ribbon windows added as separate elements, or full-height glazing in areas where sprinklers are not required. Self supporting panels are a more recent development and comprise precast panels which are stacked together in the manner of metal composite panels, with a tongue-and-groove connection between panels in the horizontal joints. These panels have the advantage of having internal insulation together with external and internal faces that require no further treatment.

Individually supported panels

This system allows narrower joints to be formed between panels than those possible in full-height panels, and allow a varied, non-rectangular layout to be used with a joint pattern independent of the backing wall. Individually supported panels use a fixing method which is similar to stone cladding panels, but with the possibility of much bigger panel sizes. Natural stone cladding is limited to sizes that can be cut from a stone block, which is usually around 2000mm x 2000mm x 2000mm (6.5ftx6.5ftx6.5ft), depending on stone type. This yields stones which are a maximum of around 1500mm x 750mm, (5ft x 2ft6in) or 1500mm x 1000mm (5ft x 3ft3in) depending on the strength of the stone. Precast concrete panels can be much larger, typically 1500mm x 3000mm (5ft x 10ft) which can be supported on stainless steel fixings back to floor

Details

1. Backing wall
2. Precast concrete panel
3. Closed cell thermal insulation
4. Vertical joint open or closed type
5. Horizontal joint (typically a lap) open or closed type
6. Internal finish
7. Window frame
8. Reinforced concrete column
9. Metal corner trim
10. Metal parapet coping
11. Concrete floor deck
12. Adjacent panel in different material
13. Waterproof membrane
14. Precast concrete coping

Section 1:10. Junction at window jamb and at parapet.

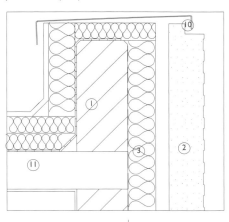

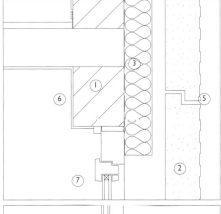

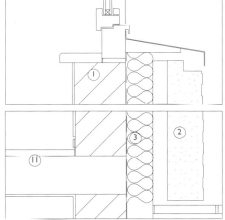

Palacio de Congresos, Santiago de Compostela, Spain. Architect: Alberto Noguerol y Pilar Diez Architects.

Plan 1:10. Panel junctions at corners.

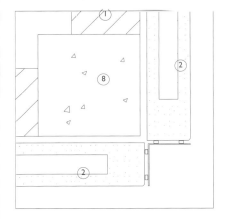

slabs and primary structure. An advantage of precast concrete over natural stone in smaller panels is that corner units and non-rectangular shaped units can be formed more easily and economically than in stone, though the number of panel types is restricted for any project in order to keep the system economic. Small precast concrete rainscreen panels are used increasingly in apartment buildings where large areas of opaque wall can be given a high degree of finish in the material while benefiting from the casting ability of the material.

Panels are most commonly fixed with stainless steel angles which are either cast-in or are bolted to the concrete. The angles are

secured to brackets fixed to a backing wall. Slotted holes provide adjustment vertically, horizontally and laterally. These panels have the advantage of being able to have a rich surface texture as a result of the casting process in an individual mould. Slots, grooves and complex profiling can be incorporated in the manner of profiled metal cladding. Backing walls are usually waterproofed in the outer face. Closed cell thermal insulation is set on the outside of this to insulate the building structure. An alternative method is to use metal foil faced insulation which is semi-rigid. The insulation is fixed directly to the blockwork backing wall, with an outer metal foil face that provides the full weather protection. Joints between strips of insulation

are sealed with adhesive foil tape.

Like stone cladding, panels are usually supported on short lengths of stainless steel angle at each floor level, back to the floor slab. This overcomes the risk of progressive collapse of a cladding panel, where a failure in one panel would cause it to drop onto the panel below, causing further collapse down the facade. Panels at floor level are fixed directly to the slab, with fixings designed so that they can take the full load of the panels immediately above, in the event of fixings to panels above failing either partially or completely.

MASONRY

(1) Masonry loadbearing walls
Brick, stone and
concrete block :
Mortars
Parapets
Cills and openings

(2) Masonry cavity walls:
Brick
Ground level
Window and door openings
Eaves and parapets

(3) Masonry cavity walls:
Stone and concrete block
Wall structures
Openings in walls

(4) Masonry cladding:
Cavity walls in framed
structures
Ground level
Window and door openings
Eaves and parapets

(5) Masonry rainscreens:
Cavity walls in framed
structures
Ground level
Window and door openings
Eaves and parapets

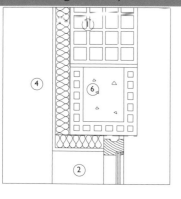

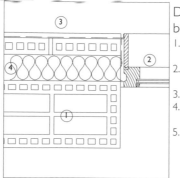

Details for hollow brick

1. Loadbearing hollow brick wall
2. Timber framed window
3. Internal finish
4. Thermal insulation
5. Hollow brick cill

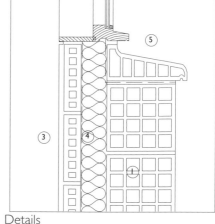

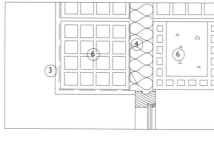

Plan 1:10. Window opening

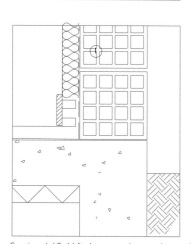

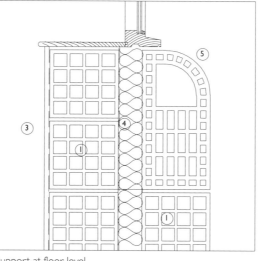

Details

6. U-shaped brick, filled with reinforced concrete
7. Waterproof membrane
8. Damp proof course (DPC)
9. Weather bar
10. Hollow brick coping
11. Roof construction
12. Rendered finish
13. Floor slab

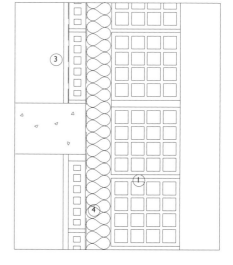

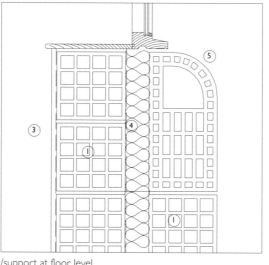

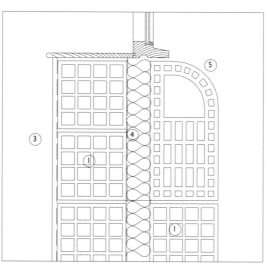

Section 1:10. Window openings and restraint/support at floor level

In masonry loadbearing construction, a complete wall is bonded together to form a single structure. Loadbearing brick walls formed with traditional sized bricks follow traditional bonding patterns which set the bricks together in a way that avoids continuity in vertical joints. In other words, each course is laid in a way that is different from the course below, in order to ensure that joints between bricks are staggered vertically. This ensures that the wall behaves structurally as a homogenous construction with discontinuous joints. Traditional brick bonds have a recognisable appearance in elevation. For example, Flemish bond has courses of alternate headers (short edge) and stretchers (long edge) set side by side. Each course

is offset from the one below to avoid a continuity of vertical joints that would weaken it structurally. English bond has alternate courses of all headers set on courses of all stretchers.

In the horizontal joints, bonds in all loadbearing materials have a continuous path from outside to inside, which reduces its resistance to water penetration. Traditionally, this is overcome by making the wall sufficiently deep to avoid the passage of water through the thickness of the wall. In contemporary construction, a vapour barrier is usually added to the inside face if the wall is dry lined, or the wall is faced internally with a waterproof render to ensure moisture does

not penetrate the joint.

In brick construction it is usually assumed that a wall around 315mm (12in), which corresponds to one brick length plus one brick width in a bond, is sufficient to resist rainwater penetration in temperate climates. This is dependent upon brick density and manufacturing dimensions, but walls of a thickness corresponding to one brick length only are usually not deemed to be thick enough, and often suffer from dampness on their internal faces if there is no damp proof membrane and/or waterproofed render on the inside face.

While loadbearing concrete block is

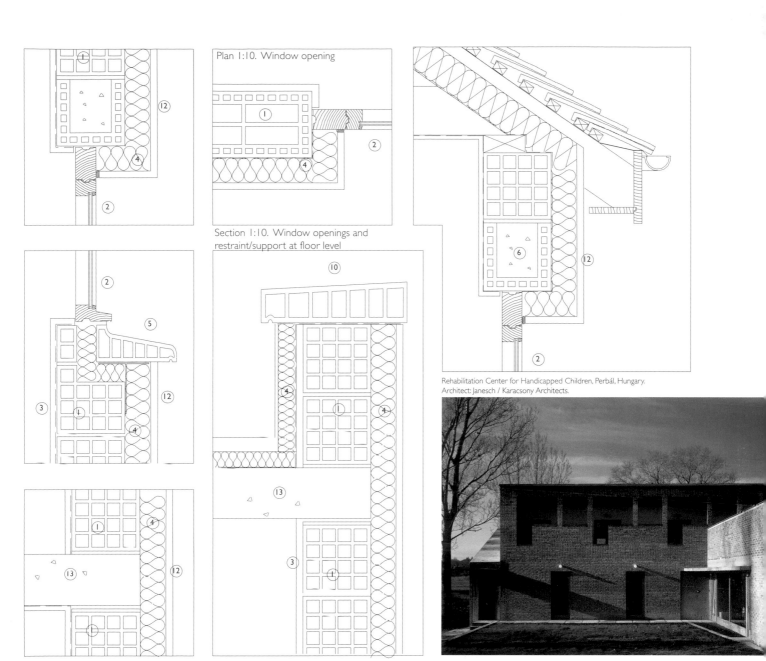

Plan 1:10. Window opening

Section 1:10. Window openings and
restraint/support at floor level

Rehabilitation Center for Handicapped Children, Perbál, Hungary.
Architect: Janesch / Karacsony Architects.

common in housing, stone is used mainly as part of a loadbearing stone wall where block or brick is the primary material. It is often the case that stone is used as a facing material to a more economic material behind. If stone is used as a loadbearing material rather than as additional cladding then its properties must be compatible with those physical properties of the backing wall.

With the increased use of thermal insulation to reduce energy consumption within buildings, thermal insulation is set on the inside face to allow the material to be visible on the outside face. However, this results in the thermal mass of the wall not being used for night time cooling. Where the internal

face of the wall is required for night time cooling, the thermal insulation can be set in the middle of the wall construction, with the leaves of brick, stone or block on either side linked by stainless steel ties to form a diaphragm wall. However, this is an unusual solution as structural discontinuity in the wall construction is less efficient from the structural point of view. As the height of the wall increases between floor slabs or between points of restraint, the thickness of the wall also increases to provide stability. An alternative to the traditional method of simply making the wall thicker is to form a diaphragm wall. Two skins of brick, typically 215mm to 315mm thick (9in-12in), are set apart with fin walls set perpendicular to the direction of

these brick walls. Concrete block walls will be typically 200mm or 300mm thick (8in or 12in).

When used internally, thermal insulation provides a full continuity between the insulated wall and insulated glazed units set into openings. The thermal insulation passes under the internal cill and is set in a way that avoids visual clumsiness that can spoil the appearance of loadbearing brick, stone and block. Internally, the insulation is finished with plaster and a projecting cill that gives a traditional visual appearance around a window.

The colour range of cut stone is very important in loadbearing stonework in order to ensure that a wall has a 'massive' appear-

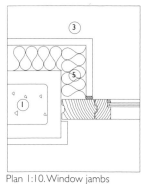

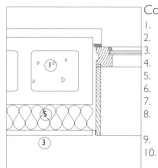

Concrete block details

1. Loadbearing block wall
2. Timber framed window
3. External render finish
4. Internal finish
5. Thermal insulation
6. Precast concrete cill
7. Precast concrete lintel
8. Damp proof course (DPC)
9. Weather bar
10. Seal

Section 1:10. Window openings

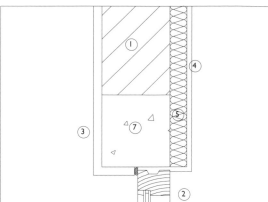

Plan 1:10. Window jambs

Section 1:10. Window openings

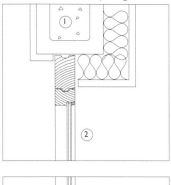

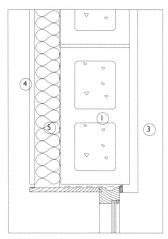

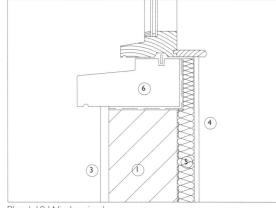

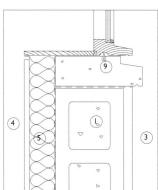

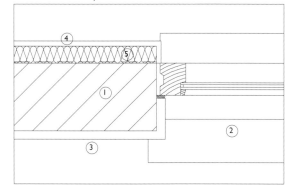

Plan 1:10. Window jambs

the dowels by means of holes drilled into the underside of the coping.

Cills and openings

Openings in loadbearing stone, brick and block have the advantage of revealing the thickness of the material, giving a massive appearance to the wall. Openings in cavity walls and cladding require corner pieces that have a joint adjacent to the corner, giving the appearance of a wall covered in a different material rather than being a surface appearing to have been carved out of solid material. However, repetition in the size and shape of corner pieces is needed in order to keep the construction as economic as possible.

Cills are formed from either the same material if stone is used for the wall, or precast concrete if the wall is made from brick or block. In common with copings, cills are sloped with a projecting edge that throws the rainwater clear of the wall beneath. A throating is also used to avoid water running back to the facade from the underside of the projecting cill. Where stone is used, the type of stone must be suitable for use as a cill. Where softer stones such as limestones and sandstones are used for the wall, stone for the coping must be sufficiently dense and durable to avoid rainwater being absorbed into the cill itself, causing staining on the top of the cill. More dense stones will absorb little water, which will instead be thrown clear

of the cill during rain. Some harder limestones and sandstones may still be suitable for use as cill pieces. Cills are usually made in single pieces, but where openings are wide, sections are set side by side with mortar joints between them. The DPC, incorporated beneath cills in all materials, drains away any water that soaks through the cill, particularly at the joints.

The heads of openings in loadbearing masonry walls are supported by lintels or arches. In traditional brick construction, a flat or curved arch is used to support the brickwork above. In concrete block construction, a reinforced concrete lintel is used, which spans the complete width of the wall, while

Isometric view of concrete block wall assembly

Plans, sections 1:10. Bedding reinforcement between courses, diaphragm wall

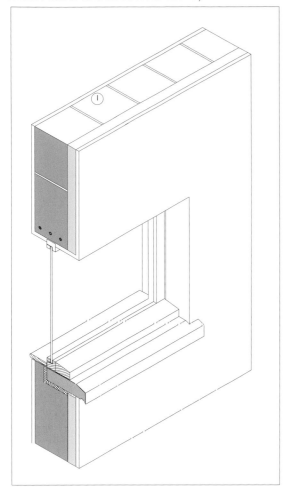

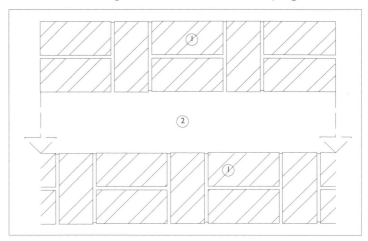

Diaphragm brick wall details
1. Loadbearing diaphragm brick wall
2. Air void or thermal insulation

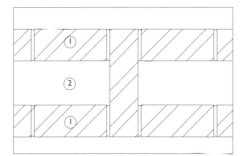

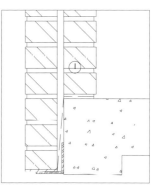

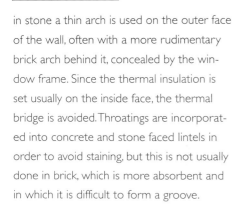

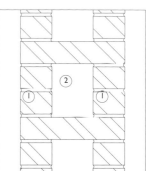

in stone a thin arch is used on the outer face of the wall, often with a more rudimentary brick arch behind it, concealed by the window frame. Since the thermal insulation is set usually on the inside face, the thermal bridge is avoided. Throatings are incorporated into concrete and stone faced lintels in order to avoid staining, but this is not usually done in brick, which is more absorbent and in which it is difficult to form a groove.

Rehabilitation Center for Handicapped Children, Perbál, Hungary.
Architect: Janesch / Karacsony Architects.

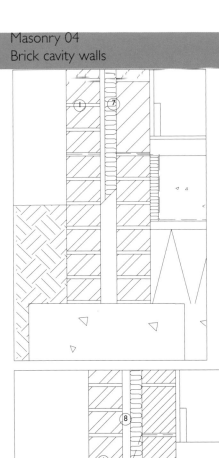

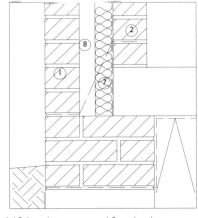

Section 1:10. Junctions at ground floor level

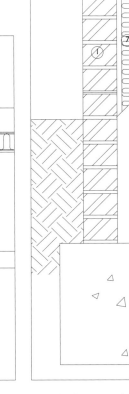

Section 1:20 Wall assembly

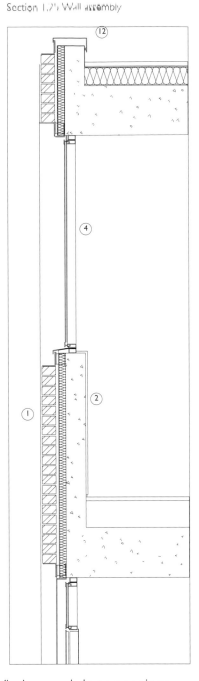

Ground level

The detailing of the DPC at ground floor level is dependent upon the difference in height between ground floor level in the building and the adjacent external level. The DPC in the outer skin is set at around 150mm above external ground level. The DPC for the internal skin is set at the same level if the step up from outside to inside is around 150mm. If the difference between outside and inside levels is around 300mm/12in then the DPC is stepped up from outer skin to inner skin in the same place but a separate DPC is added to the inner skin at the same level as the bottom of the cavity tray. The aim of the damp proofing is to provide a continuity of protection from

underneath the ground floor or lowest basement slab up into the wall construction.

The cavity is filled below ground floor level to avoid it filling with water which would eventually damage the construction, particularly from freezing in winter in temperate climates. Until recently, thermal insulation was usually terminated at ground floor level. More recently, the thermal insulation continues down below ground where it is continuous with thermal insulation set on top of or beneath the floor slab to provide a completely insulated building enclosure.

Window and door openings

Since a window or door frame has a profile which is the same on all four sides, with an external modification for the cill, the profile of the opening into which it fits must be consistent on all sides. Visual considerations are equally important in the detailing of cavity wall openings. The depths of the reveal can make the outer skin appear more 'massive' if the reveal is made at least one brick deep or more like a thin skin if the window is set forward of the reveal. Where a load-bearing wall can incorporate a structural brick arch, this is much more difficult in a cavity wall. This is because the outer and inner skins of a cavity wall are kept separate, except where they are bridged by lintels.

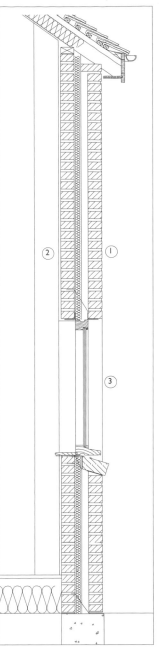

Moderna Museet, Stockholm. Architect: Rafael Moneo Arquitectos.

Details

1. Outer brick skin
2. Inner blockwork or brick skin
3. Timber framed window
4. Timber cill
5. Cavity closer
6. Internal plaster finish or dry lining/drywall
7. Thermal insulation in cavity
8. Air cavity (sometimes omitted where insulation fills cavity)
9. Inner concrete lintel or beam
10. Pressed steel lintel
11. Steel angle
12. Metal coping
13. Precast concrete cill
14. Damp proof course (DPC)
15. Brick cill
16. Movement joint

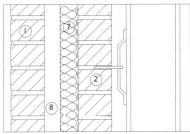

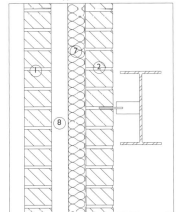

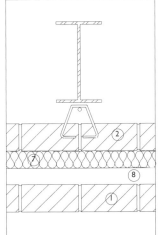

Section 1:10.
Support of outer leaf at floor slab and at ground level

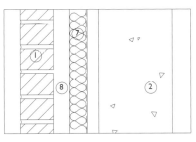

Because they are linked only at these points, the lintel needs to be a separate structural element which supports both skins without exerting lateral forces in the adjacent brickwork, where cracking could occur in both skins. For this reason, simply supported lintels are used, which exert balanced loads on both skins. Both reinforced concrete and steel types are used, which have the advantage of supporting a course of bricks to give the appearance of a flat arch. Reinforced concrete lintels appear as beams visible in both elevation and on the soffit (underside), while steel lintels are visible only on the soffit of the opening, making it clearly visible that the bricks across the top of the opening on the outer face are not self supporting unlike loadbearing wall construction. For this reason brickwork supported by a steel lintel is often not set on edge to form an arch, but is coursed the same as the brickwork above, since any arch supported by a steel lintel is decorative. However, an advantage of the steel lintel is that it can incorporate a cavity tray, with rainwater being drained through weep holes in vertical joints in the bottom course.

Lintels are supported on both skins at their bearing points. A reinforced concrete lintel spans across both skins either in a profile that also forms a cavity tray (A) for wide spans or as a flat lintel (B) for short spans. The lintel in (A) has a beam section supporting the inner skin which provides the spanning element and a toe supporting the outer skin. A DPC is set onto the lintel to drain water. The lintel in (B) also requires a DPC which is set above the lintel. In both cases thermal insulation is set on the inside face of the wall to avoid a thermal bridge. Steel lintels can be used either as a pressed mild steel lintel which has a profile for supporting both skins, or as reinforced concrete lintel with a stainless steel shelf angle bolted to it (D). In (C) the lintel has a DPC set on top of the profile formed by the lintel where the inner block has no structural function but is instead used to infill the gap and provide a background for plaster. In lintel (D) the stainless steel angle has a DPC set onto

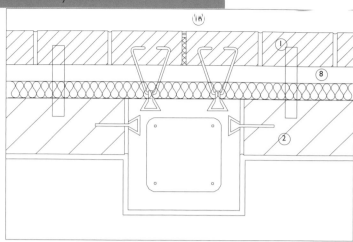

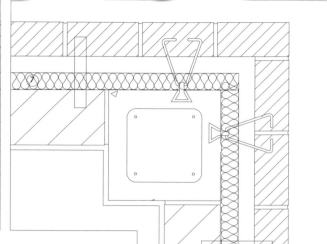

Details

1. Outer brick skin
2. Inner blockwork or brick skin
3. Timber framed window
4. Timber cill
5. Cavity closer
6. Internal plaster finish or dry lining/drywall
7. Thermal insulation in cavity

8. Air cavity (sometimes omitted where insulation fills cavity)
9. Inner concrete lintel
10. Pressed steel lintel or beam
11. Steel angle
12. Metal coping
13. Precast concrete cill
14. Damp proof course (DPC)
15. Brick cill
16. Movement joint

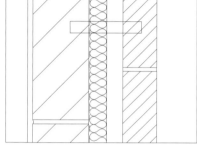

Plan 1:10. Corner conditions

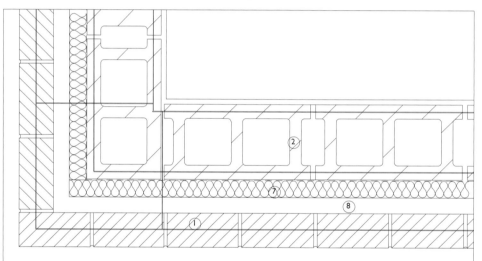

it. The angle supports the outer skin, while the reinforced concrete inner beam supports both inner and outer skins.

Eaves and parapets

At the eaves, the bottom of a pitched roof terminates against the top of a brick cavity wall. While there are many variations for the roof itself, the top of the wall maintains a consistent principle of closing the cavity at the top with a brick or block that allows the load from the roof structure to be supported on the inner skin. Alternatively, the roof structure may be supported on a column set into the inner skin of the wall or on blockwork piers, also forming part of the inner skin. The closing of the cavity wall at the

top allows for continuity of thermal insulation from cavity wall to roof structure while allowing the roof construction to be ventilated where required, and the top of the cavity in the wall to be ventilated. The top of the wall usually has plastic spacers set into the horizontal or vertical joints to ensure that air movement can occur within the cavity. A DPC is set on the underside of the brick or block that closes the cavity to ensure continuity between the damp proof membrane on the external face of the inner skin and the waterproofing layer of the roof.

Parapets are closed at the top by a coping, usually in reinforced concrete or stone. A DPC is set beneath the coping to stop the

passage of water downwards. Below this, rainwater can enter the cavity from both inner and outer skins and this is prevented by extending the waterproof layer from the roof up the side of the inner skin up to coping level. Thermal insulation is usually continued up the inside of the cavity wall as well as up the external face of the inner skin to avoid a thermal bridge through the inner skin.

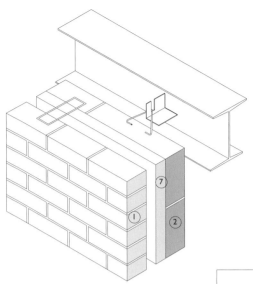

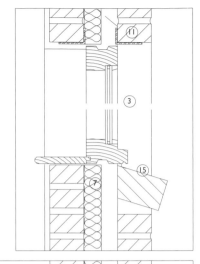

Isometric views of wall assembly,
1. with steel support, 2. with concrete support

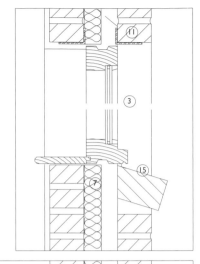

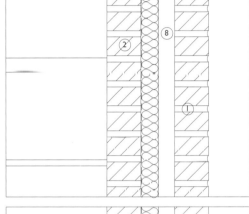

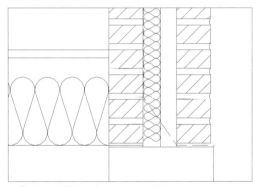

Section 1:10. Junctions at ground floor
level and at window

Moderna Museet, Stockholm. Architect: Rafael Moneo Arquitectos.

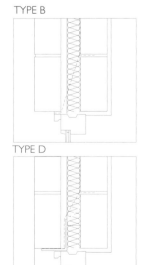

TYPE A   TYPE B

TYPE C   TYPE D

Section 1:10. Typical window at cill and head

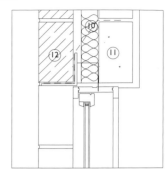
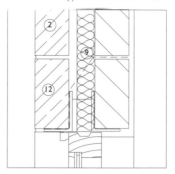
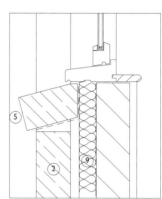
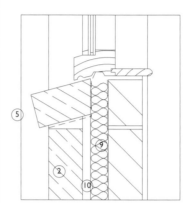

Section 1:10. Junction at ground floor level

Plan 1:10. Typical window jamb

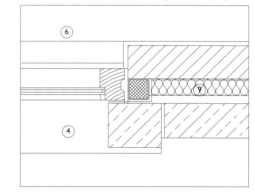

Details

1. Stone or concrete coping
2. Outer stone skin with brick backing shown to create deep window reveals or where required structurally.
3. Inner block skin
4. Timber framed window / door
5. Stone or precast concrete cill
6. Timber inner cill
7. Cavity closer
8. Internal plaster finish or dry lining/dry wall
9. Thermal insulation in cavity

The principles of cavity wall design are set out in the previous text on brick cavity walls. The same principles can be applied for use when stone and concrete blockwork are used to form an outer skin.

When stone is used, it can be used either as an outer skin approximately 100mm/4in thick, or with thinner stone that is bonded to brickwork that together forms a 'composite' outer skin. When used as a 100mm/4in thick skin in order to be self-supporting, the stone becomes expensive, so sandstones and limestones are most commonly used. Composite-type outer skins suit stone that is 40mm to 50mm thick (1.5in-2.0in), bonded to a 100mm/4in wide brick skin. This method suits

granites and denser limestones.

In single outer skins of stone, the material is ventilated on both sides, allowing it to dry out easily, avoiding a situation where stone would dry from only the outer face, which would draw dirt and dust out into the outside face.

The biggest difference in detailing between brick cavity walls and stone / block cavity walls is that there are fewer joints in stone / block due to their large size. This means that there are fewer opportunities to design a damp proof course (DPC) with floor slabs, for example, particularly where shelf angles are used. The smaller unit size of

brick makes it a very flexible material when detailing; stone / block requires careful co-ordination of stone / block size and floor to floor heights to allow for windows to be suitably placed. For this reason, alternating bands of thick and thin stone are used in coursing. This allows horizontal joint lines to be provided at shelf angles, cavity trays and DPCs at ground level without disturbing the stone pattern with additional horizontal joints. Unlike open jointed stone cladding, where the mortar is omitted, the mortar and joint profile have a big visual impact.

Cavity walls in framed structures

Loadbearing cavity walls used to support two storey structures on their inner skins are

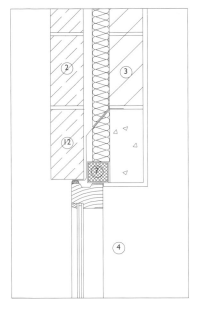

Town Hall, Valdemqueda, Spain. Architect: García de Paredes/Pedrosa Architects.

10. Air cavity (sometimes omitted where insulation fills cavity)
11. Inner precast concrete lintel
12. Outer precast concrete lintel or stone flat arch
13. Damp proof course (DPC)
14. Movement joint
15. Timber framed inner skin with quilt insulation
16. Cement fill
17. Foundation
18. Vertical DPC
19. Structural column
20. Floor construction

Section 1:10.
Typical window at cill and head, parapet and eaves to pitched roof

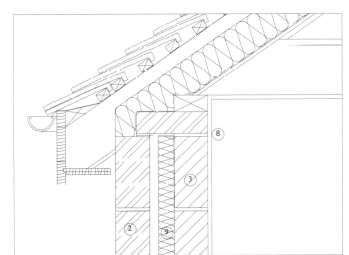

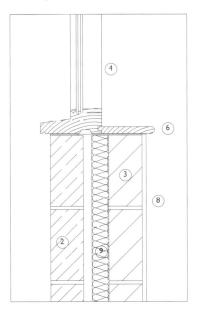

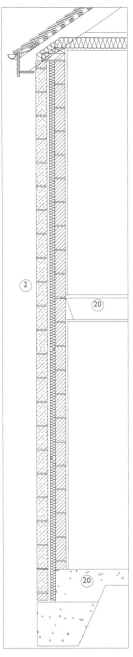

very common in housing construction in Europe and North America. Vertical movement joints are provided at around 7500mm/25ft centres, or else are avoided altogether in the construction by keeping lengths of wall within these dimensions. When cavity walls are used with large scale building frames in either steel or concrete, the inner leaf is no longer loadbearing and instead the complete wall construction forms a cladding to the frame. When reinforced concrete frames are used, the junction between inner skin, typically concrete block or terracotta block, is straightforward with a gap between the two to allow for structural movement in the frame. Stainless steel sliding anchors are used either in the

sides of the inner skin panel where it meets the column, or at the head where it meets the floor slab. The outer skin runs continuously in front of it. The situation is more complicated with a steel frame, where the column needs to be protected from corrosion from water vapour in the cavity. Typically the column is painted to form a protective coating and thermal insulation is set across the face of the steelwork to provide a continuity of thermal insulation. Sometimes the outer skin is restrained with cavity ties fixed to the face of the reinforced concrete or steel column. This is particularly useful when forming a movement joint in lengths of brickwork, or movement joints that form part of the building structure which typically

occur at columns in the building frame. The vertical movement joint is filled with two part polysulphide sealant that also matches the colour of the mortar as closely as possible and provides a seal that can accommodate the structural movement within the cavity wall.

Ground level

An essential design consideration at ground level is to provide a DPC at a minimum 150mm/6in above ground floor level with a horizontal joint that can be accommodated within the design. Granite is often used below DPC level to avoid staining from rain splashing from the adjacent ground and from dust and damage in urban locations.

Section 1:10.
Typical window at cill

Plan 1:10, Typical connection
or restraint to primary structure

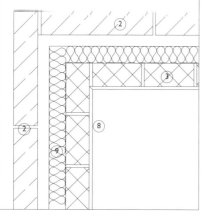

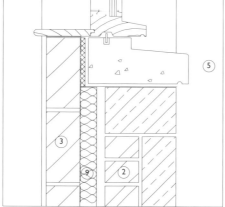

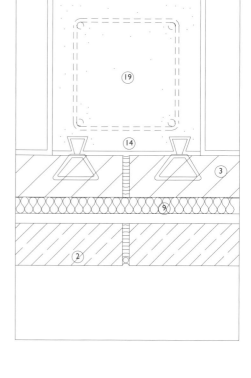

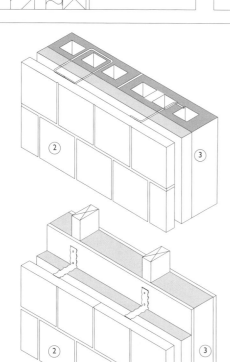

Isometric view of wall assembly.

Details

1. Stone or concrete coping
2. Outer stone skin with brick backing shown to create deep window reveals or where required structurally.
3. Inner block skin
4. Timber framed window / door
5. Stone or precast concrete cill
6. Timber inner cill
7. Cavity closer
8. Internal plaster finish or dry lining/dry wall
9. Thermal insulation in cavity
10. Air cavity (sometimes omitted where insulation fills cavity)
11. Inner precast concrete lintel

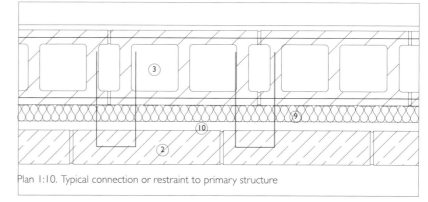

Plan 1:10. Typical connection or restraint to primary structure

need a joint for expansion at the head. A compressible durable seal is used, recessed from the face of the outer skin to avoid a colour clash with the mortar below. Stainless steel angles with slotted connections are also used to restrain masonry at the head, or even a stainless steel channel if the underside of the concrete is revealed. When the concrete slab soffit is concealed with additional cladding, a horizontal joint in the outer skin is usually placed to align with the cladding to avoid the appearance of the stone disappearing behind the soffit. The outer skin continues with another course to close against the slab soffit. Where a downstand beam is used to support the concrete roof slab above, the beam is usually aligned with the inner skin of

the cavity wall. A stepped DPC is set the other way round from its usual position, draining from the outer leaf to the inner leaf, but water running down the underside of the DPC is drained harmlessly down the outer face of the inner skin. If timber is used in a projecting flat roof the DPC is set on top of the wall, on which roof timbers are supported. A continuity of thermal insulation is provided. The timber roof structure can also be ventilated to allow it to be kept dry while maintaining thermal insulation.

For parapets the inner skin is thickened up when used as a balustrade. A handrail on top of the coping is fixed by drilling through the top and bolting it to the inner skin

beneath. The coping is cut to receive the balustrade or handrail, unless the uprights supporting the handrail pass between the joints. The adjacent area of flat roof or gutter usually has a waterproofing layer returning up the wall, regardless of the roof finish. The waterproofing layer is set into horizontal joints in outer masonry skin. A metal flashing is set into the same horizontal joint and is set over the top of the waterproofing to protect it from damage. Metal copings are used increasingly on parapets in order to match the appearance of windows and doors, particularly where metal cills are used. The same principles apply as for concrete copings, with a DPC set on top of the masonry wall. Drips are formed on either

Town Hall, Valdemqueda, Spain. Architect: García de Paredes/Pedrosa Architects.

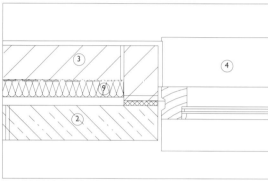

12. Outer precast concrete lintel or stone flat arch
13. Damp proof course (DPC)
14. Movement joint
15. Timber framed inner skin with quilt insulation
16. Cement fill
17. Foundation
18. Vertical DPC
19. Structural column
20. Floor construction

Section 1:10.
Typical window at cill and head

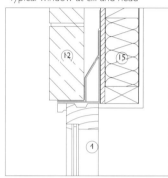

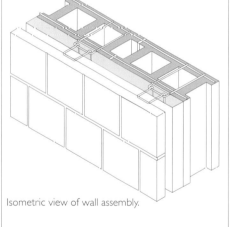

Isometric view of wall assembly.

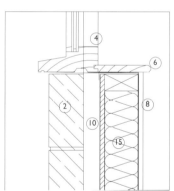

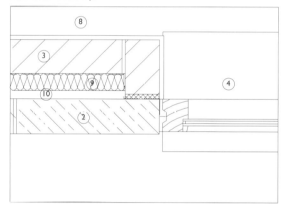

Plan 1:10. Window jambs

side of the vertical face to ensure that water is thrown clear of the wall. For all parapets, the waterproofing layer is continued up the wall to become continuous with the DPC in low parapets. For high parapet walls, a stepped DPC is used to drain water back to the inner skin to ensure that water inside this part of the cavity wall is drained immediately, especially in very exposed conditions. A stepped DPC is used instead of a regular flat DPC under the coping.

Town Hall, Valdemqueda, Spain. Architect: García de Paredes/Pedrosa Architects.

Section 1:25.
Typical stone carrier system
Key shown on previous page

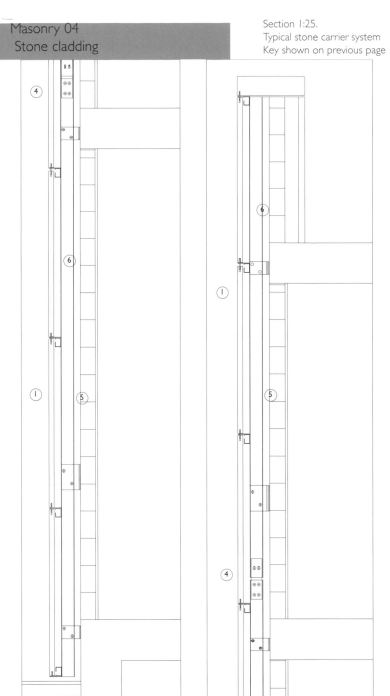

City Hall, Murcia, Spain. Architect: Rafael Moneo Arquitectos.

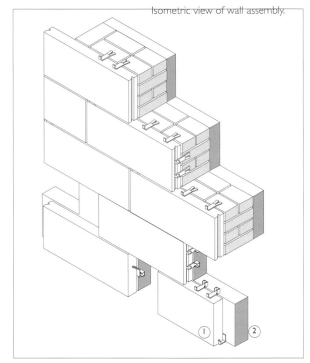

Isometric view of wall assembly.

(0.118in) diameter for stone up to 30mm (1.2in) thick and 5mm (0.2in) for stone of greater thicknesses.

Face fixings are normally used with marble and granite. The bolts function as both loadbearing and restraint fixings and are set away from the corners in the manner of bolt fixed glazing. A bolt is fixed in each corner, usually at a distance equal to three times the stone thickness but to a maximum distance of around 75mm (3in) from the corner. Smaller stones are fixed with fewer fixings, and triangular panels usually have a fixing in each corner only.

Fixings used to support stones that clad

soffits, such as the underside of a concrete slab, are suspended from bolts or hangers which slide into anchorages cast into the supporting structure.

Stone cladding to precast concrete panels

Any of the stones listed at the beginning of this section can be used as a facing to precast concrete panels, but granite is most commonly used due to its higher strength, allowing it to be used relatively thinly. Thicker sandstones and limestones are also used, however. Stone is fixed to concrete panels with dowel pin fixings which are inclined at 45° to 60° to suit the size of stone and holding it in place. Pins are usually set at around

200mm (8in) centres both vertically and horizontally with a pin thickness of around 5mm. 50% of dowels are set in each direction to provide a balanced support. Each dowel has a flexible rubber-based washer around 3mm (0.118in) thick to allow for the movement between stone and the concrete background. The dowel penetrates 2/3 the thickness of the stone and around 60mm - 75mm into the concrete (2.3in-3in).

Joints

Joints are either of closed or open type. Closed joints use either mortar or proprietary sealant. Closed joints are used where the cladding is supported at each floor level on stainless steel angles with jointed stones.

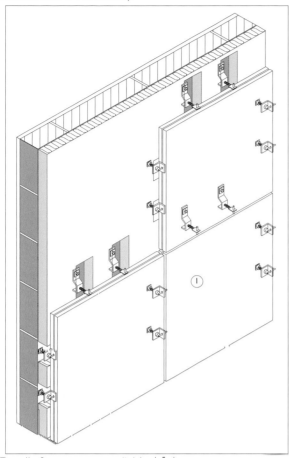

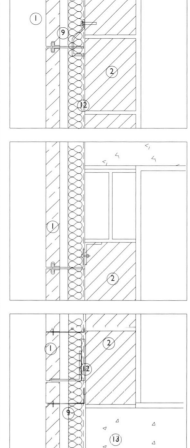

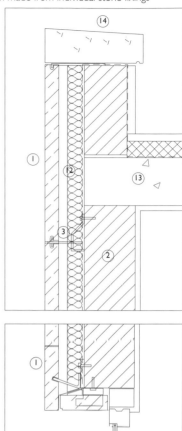

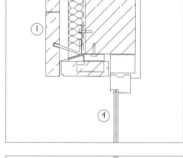

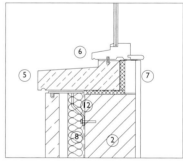

Details for stone on individual fixings

1. Stone panel
2. Backing wall, typically concrete block
3. Stainless steel fixings (a wide range is available)
4. Timber framed window
5. Stone cill
6. Timber inner cill
7. Internal plaster finish or dry lining/drywall
8. Thermal insulation in cavity
9. Stainless steel restraint at each floor level
10. Air cavity
11. Precast concrete lintel
12. Waterproof membrane
13. Floor slab
14. Stone coping

With open jointed stones, each panel is individually supported in a rainscreen construction, where rainwater passing through the joints is drained away down either the back of the stones or down the face of the backing wall.

Closed joints

Closed joints need to be loadbearing and watertight and must also accommodate relative movements of cladding and supporting building structure. The types of jointing or pointing (the outer finish of mortar or sealant) will depend on the type, size, thickness and surface finish of cladding units. Stones are not usually butted up against one another, since any movement of the unit or

of the structure cannot be accommodated, causing damage to the stones.

Joints in sandstone and limestone are usually filled with cement/sand mortar or cement/sand/lime mortar. Granite and slate typically use proprietary sealant, such as two-part polysulphide. Mortar used for pointing is made frost resistant when used in temperate climates, and of similar strength to the jointing mortar, which is the structural mortar behind. Neither mortar should be stronger than the stone. For limestone and sandstone a mortar of 1/1/5 for cement/lime/sand is typically used, or 1/2/8 for cement/lime/crushed stone particles, where the colour of the mortar is blended

with the crushed stone.

For narrow joints used with granite or slate, a high cement-to-sand ratio is used. Joints wider than around 4mm are filled with a weaker mix to reduce shrinkage cracks. The maximum widths of mortar filled joints are around 12mm (0.5in) but sealant filled joints can be up to around 30mm (1.2in), depending on the proprietary product used. Joint widths are usually a function of the cutting tolerance of the stone, around 2mm difference in the cut line of the stone, depending on stone type and the cutting machine used. Modern machines can cut stones to within 1mm accuracy. Joint widths of 4mm are common, but this can rise to a maximum

City Hall, Murcia, Spain. Architect: Rafael Moneo Arquitectos.

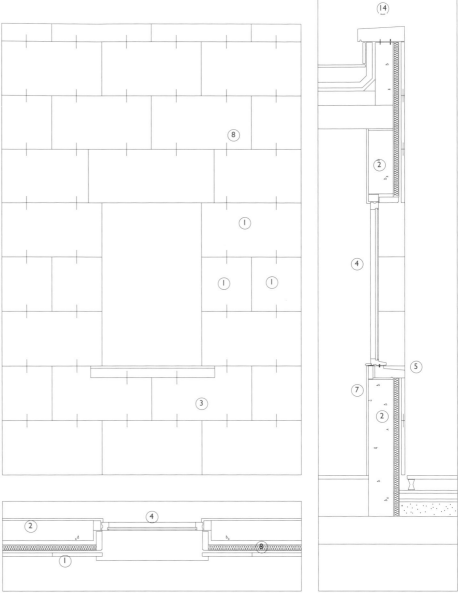

Plan and section 1:10.
Typical stone carrier system made from individual stone fixings

of 12mm when required for visual reasons, particularly when the joint is recessed. Granite, slates and hard limestones and sandstones can have a joint width at a minimum of 3mm, while soft sandstones and limestones can be laid with a minimum 5mm joint. When a proprietary sealant is used, the minimum joint width for all stone types is usually around 5mm.

Movement joints

Horizontal movement joints are used to deal mainly with floor slab deflections, and to a lesser extent vertical shortening, in the structural frame. This horizontal joint is usually provided at slab level, where the stone cladding is supported from either short

lengths of stainless steel angle, or a continuous shelf angle. The joint occurs immediately below the stainless steel angle, where vertical deflection will occur. Horizontal movement joints can be set at intervals of two storeys if the stone and support brackets or frame can be designed to span the height. The joint width is usually a minimum of 15mm, but 20mm to 25mm (0.8in-1in) are common with reinforced concrete structures. The joint is formed either as a sealant or as a step in the stone, where the upper stone projects forward of the stone below to conceal the wider joint. In both joint types the joint is made watertight where closed joints are used, and an open joint where rainscreen cladding principles are used.

Vertical movement joints are provided to deal with racking in the structure as well as movements in the cladding itself. Where movement joints occur in the building structure, usually following a continuous vertical line where it intersects with the facade, a vertical movement joint is provided in the facade in the same location. The distance between joints is typically at around 6 metres in a continuous run of stone cladding with closed joints. The joint width corresponds to the expected movement in the cladding, but where sealed joints are used, the joint width is dependent on the amount of movement that the sealant is required to accommodate. Minimum widths of vertical movement joints are around 10mm (0.5in).

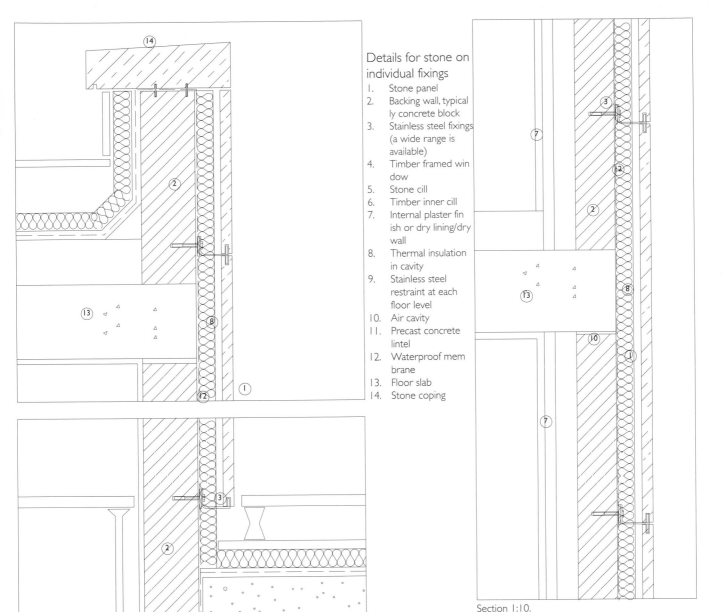

Details for stone on individual fixings

1. Stone panel
2. Backing wall, typically concrete block
3. Stainless steel fixings (a wide range is available)
4. Timber framed window
5. Stone cill
6. Timber inner cill
7. Internal plaster finish or dry lining/dry wall
8. Thermal insulation in cavity
9. Stainless steel restraint at each floor level
10. Air cavity
11. Precast concrete lintel
12. Waterproof membrane
13. Floor slab
14. Stone coping

Section 1:10.
Typical stone carrier system made from individual stone fixings

Vertical movement joints are extended into parapets and copings.

Stone finishes

Granites, limestones, sandstones and slates are using an increasingly wide range of finishes, with finishes associated with one stone type being used for another. The main finishes are as follows: A rubbed finish is a smooth finish made by rubbing stone with an abrasive material (typically used for limestone and sandstone); a honed finish has a dull polish (used for all types); a polished surface has a high gloss (typically used for granite and hard limestone); a flamed finish is obtained by passing a hot flame over the stone surface (typically used for granite and slate), a riven finish, where the stone is cut on its cleavage plane (typically used for slate, sandstone or limestone) and tooled, where the material is worked, leaving tool marks and is used mainly on sandstone or limestone. In addition, stones can be filled with cements or proprietary fillers to conceal natural voids in the stone. The surface is then coated or polished.

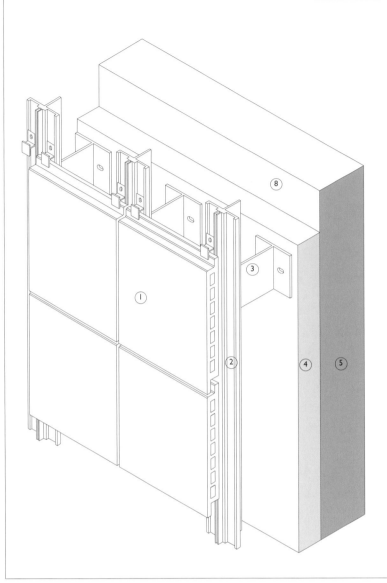

Isometric view of wall assembly.

Potsdamer Platz, Berlin. Architect: Renzo Piano Building Workshop.

The essential principles of rainscreen cladding are discussed in the section on metal rainscreens. Terracotta rainscreens have developed into patented proprietary systems from prototypes within the last 10 years. Over that time the sizes of terracotta panels have increased and fixing systems have developed for use as solar shading screens to glazed walls as part of an overall rainscreen system for a building facade. Hollow terracotta sections are reinforced with aluminium sections set into them to form louvred screens that can match with adjacent areas of cladding. Terracotta is fixed either on rails, into aluminium or stainless steel panels, or on individual brackets like masonry cladding with concealed fixings. Vertically-set or horizontal-ly-set rails are used to suit a range of joint arrangements that imitate traditional masonry bonds, or can be stack bonded in the manner of wall tiling or glass blocks. Terracotta has been developed for use in rainscreens both from building blocks and bricks, as used in loadbearing masonry construction, and from decorative tiles, where many of the glazed finishes are derived. Recently developed systems have interlocking panels, to provide crisp joints, and double wall sections to provide long spanning tiles with high flexural strength, or modulus of rupture, combined with lightness in weight. The range of glazed finishes has developed considerably in the past few years to give a very wide range of textures and colour mixes derived from contemporary pottery.

Manufacture of terracotta panels

Terracotta is made from natural clay that is extruded and fired in a kiln. Powdered clay is mixed with water in the factory to achieve a controlled level of water content. It is then extruded through dies that draw the material along a conveyor belt where it is wire cut to the required length. The use of dies makes the manufacture of terracotta panels very flexible, giving it the ability to make new shapes and sections for each new project with relative ease. The die creates different heights and depths of block, with hollowing out of the interior to keep the material relatively light and easy to handle, allowing it to

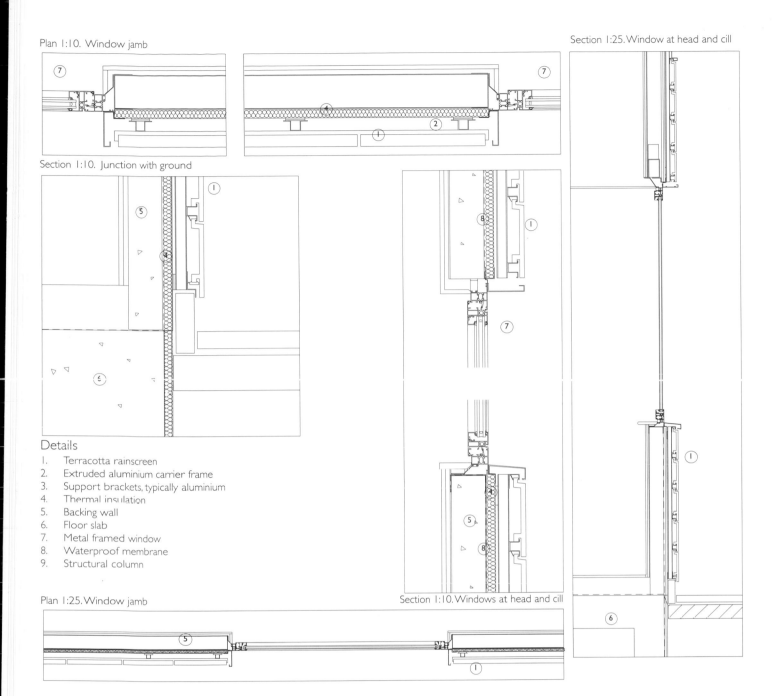

Plan 1:10. Window jamb

Section 1:25. Window at head and cill

Section 1:10. Junction with ground

Details

1. Terracotta rainscreen
2. Extruded aluminium carrier frame
3. Support brackets, typically aluminium
4. Thermal insulation
5. Backing wall
6. Floor slab
7. Metal framed window
8. Waterproof membrane
9. Structural column

Plan 1:25. Window jamb

Section 1:10. Windows at head and cill

be made in long pieces if required. The extruding process gives flexibility to the material that is similar to the creation of aluminium sections for glazed walls and windows. When the material is extruded and cut it is dried and fired in kilns of different types depending on the tile size and shape. Some terracotta panels are machined for firing in order to provide the precise profile needed for the fixing system as well as to provide precise smaller joint widths between panels.

Because terracotta panels have two extruded edges and two cut edges, it is important in arranging panels to avoid a cut edge being revealed at a corner. This is

because the surface finish and colour of the end face will not match that of the front face. The ends of extruded terracotta differ from terracotta and fired clay bricks in this respect. The ends of panels are usually concealed with aluminium trims, sometimes at the corners but typically around window openings.

Corner pieces

Special shapes can be formed by hand to match with the standard extruded tiles, such as corner pieces and decorative elements. Corner pieces are made by pressing, usually with a maximum length of 150mm (6in) on one leg and 300mm (12in) on the other leg. Large corner pieces are made by

hand by joining two sections together, but these currently produce less reliable results that can lack a straight and crisp edge. Manufacturers often provide extruded cill sections for parapets and window sections to suit wall constructions of 300mm to 500mm (12in-20in) wide. These have slopes to either one side or to both sides from the middle of the extrusion. The fired terracotta is either left in its natural colour or is glazed with a wide range of glazes. A glazed finish can give the material more visual sparkle by making the material more reflective, which also provides better durability from staining. However, water absorption of regular terracotta panels is between 3% and 6%, with a density of around 2000kg/m³, making the use of

TIMBER

Section 1:10. Junction with floor slabs

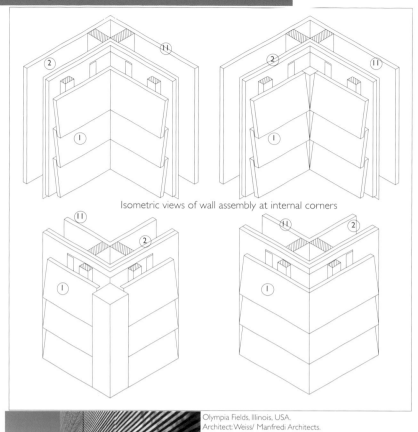

Isometric views of wall assembly at internal corners

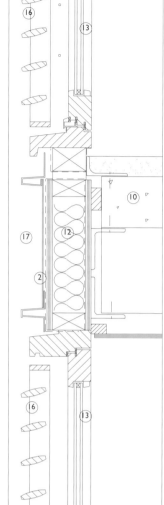

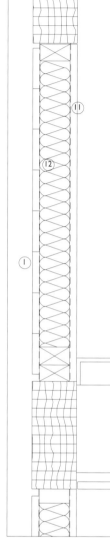

Olympia Fields, Illinois, USA.
Architect: Weiss/ Manfredi Architects.

Details

1. Timber boards
2. Plywood sheathing
3. Timber studs
4. Timber rail
5. Breather membrane
6. Foundation
7. Damp proof course
8. Vapour barrier
9. Timber floor
10. Concrete floor
11. Internal finish
12. Thermal insulation quilt set within timber frame
13. Timber framed window/door
14. Timber cill
15. Air gap
16. Sliding timber louvre panel
17. Metal facing
18. External plywood facing
19. Cover strip
20. External floor deck
21. External glass wall in twin wall
22. Structural timber frame

upper board lapped over the top of the board below to protect it from rainwater ingress. Shiplapping can be assisted by the use of 'feathered' or wedge-shaped boards to give the lapping a more elegant appearance. Tongue-and-groove boards are used to give a continuous flat appearance, while having the advantage of locking boards together into a continuous plate-like structure. Boards are typically around 20mm (0.75in) thick, made as long as possible at around 3000mm - 3500mm (10ft-11ft6in), to avoid vertical joints which are a potential source of rainwater penetration except in rainscreen configuration. Where tongue-and-groove boards are used, the groove is set on the underside to avoid water accumulating when the boards

are set horizontally or diagonally. Where tongue-and-groove boards are set vertically, the groove is set away from the prevailing wind direction to avoid windblown rain being blown into the joint. Joints between boards are never sealed along their long edges with silicone or mastic sealants as this prevents the timber from drying properly, which would cause the material to deteriorate and eventually rot. However, sealants are used on the ends of timber boards when the complete external surface is sealed with paint.

Cladding panels and rainscreens

Timber cladding to a platform frame or a balloon frame is continuous, forming an

integral part of the wall structure. In contrast, timber cladding panels are fixed to building frames in reinforced concrete, steel and timber. In this application, cladding panels follow the principle of other forms of cladding, requiring pre-fabrication of panels and allowance for structural movement in the supporting frame associated with larger-scale structures. Cladding panels can also be faced with plywood rather than timber boards, in rainscreen applications. Because of the higher moisture movement associated with timber than with other materials, junctions between cladding panels require allowance for movement as a result of changing moisture levels in the material.

TIMBER

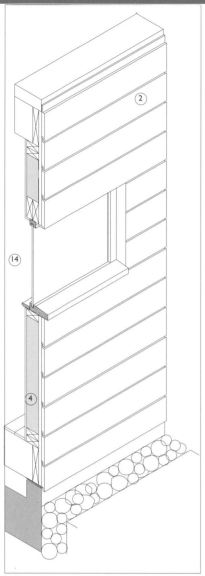

Isometric view of wall assembly

Section 1:10. Parapet

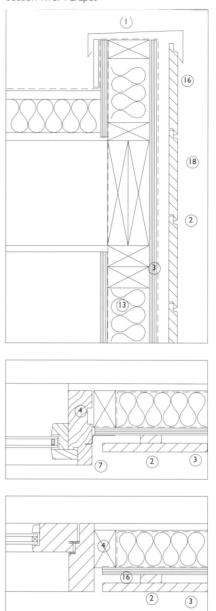

Plan 1:10. Window jambs

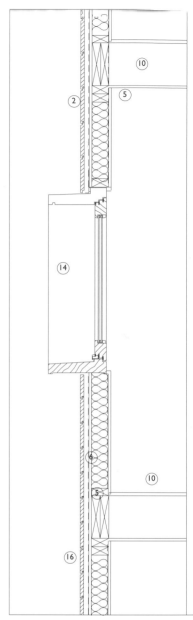

Section 1:25. Window opening

Timber cladding has traditionally been used on loadbearing timber framed walls, as discussed in this section. Its more recent application as cladding panels and as rain-screens is discussed in the second section of this chapter. There are two traditional generic forms of timber frame that use small section timbers to form framed loadbearing walls: the platform frame and the balloon frame. More historical types that use large timber sections with an infill in timber or another material are not discussed here, as their application is currently very limited. Both the platform frame and the balloon frame are based on softwood sawn timber sections around 100mmx50mm (4inx2in). These are economic, and set at close centres

of around 400mm (16in) in order to be a multiple dimension of plywood sheets and related board materials used to form the sheathing for the walls and floor decking. Since the floor joists are set at the same centres as the vertical studs, board materials are used for the floor decking in the same size. The platform frame comprises studs spanning from floor to floor, with the timber floor structure being supported at each storey height set of timber frames. The balloon frame, which is now used less, is enjoying a revival in light gauge steel sections. This method has vertical framing members which are continuous, with the intermediary floors being supported by the wall running continuously past it.

Timber frames

Timber frames comprise vertical sections called 'studs' fixed to horizontal members called 'rails'. The studs run vertically continuously, with discontinuous horizontal members which are called 'noggins'. The outer face of the timber frame is clad with plywood sheathing to provide lateral bracing, typically 12mm-18mm thick (0.5in-0.75in), depending on the structural requirement of stiffening the frame. Timber boards can also be used as sheathing, this is an expensive solution. Framing members are typically formed from 100x50mm (4inx2in) softwood sections at 400mm (16in) vertical centres which are nailed together. Mild steel corner

Olympia Fields, Illinois, USA. Architect: Weiss/ Manfredi Architects.

Details

1. Metal parapet flashing
2. Timber boards
3. Plywood sheathing
4. Timber studs
5. Timber rail
6. Breather membrane
7. Window flashing
8. Damp proof course
9. Vapour barrier
10. Timber floor
11. Concrete ground slab
12. Internal plaster finish or dry lining/dry wall
13. Thermal insulation quilt set within timber frame
14. Timber framed window/door
15. Timber cill
16. Air gap

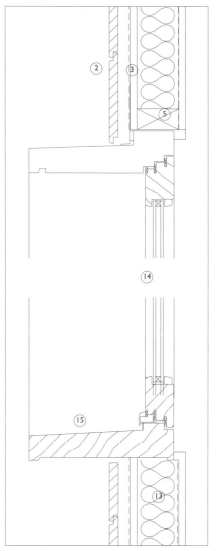

Section 1:10.
Floor junction, window opening

Plan 1:25. Window openings

brackets and cleats are commonly used to make the connections more reliable and easy to form, either on-site or in a workshop. Voids between the framing members are filled with thermal insulation. A breather membrane is then fixed to the face of the sheathing layer. This provides a waterproof barrier which also allows the vapour to escape to allow the timber wall to release and absorb moisture with changes in the weather. Outer timber cladding boards are then fixed on the outside of the breather membrane.

When timber cladding is used on timber frames, the softwood stud walls that form the wall structure can use the timber

cladding to stiffen the wall. Traditionally, this has been done by fixing the boarding directly to the timber frame, with a breather membrane set between the frame and the timber boards to allow the outer cladding to 'breathe', or dry out and absorb moisture, in response to the changes in weather conditions. Alternatively, the timber boards are fixed to battens which are set forward of the breather membrane, or waterproofing layer, to ensure that the timber is ventilated on all sides. When battens are used, the timber boards are less able to stiffen the frame if the battens are not set in alignment with every stud forming the frame of the wall behind.

The inside face of the timber framed wall has a continuous vapour barrier, typically thick polythene sheet, set onto it, in temperate climates, on the 'warm in winter' side of the wall. The inner face of the wall is then finished with plasterboard (drywall) to provide an internal finish.

Ground level

This text focuses on different conditions at ground level, upper floor levels and at roof level. The lightweight nature of timber cladding has led to its use with a raised timber ground floor, often with no concrete ground slab. This makes the junction with the ground quite different from those of the other materials described in this book.

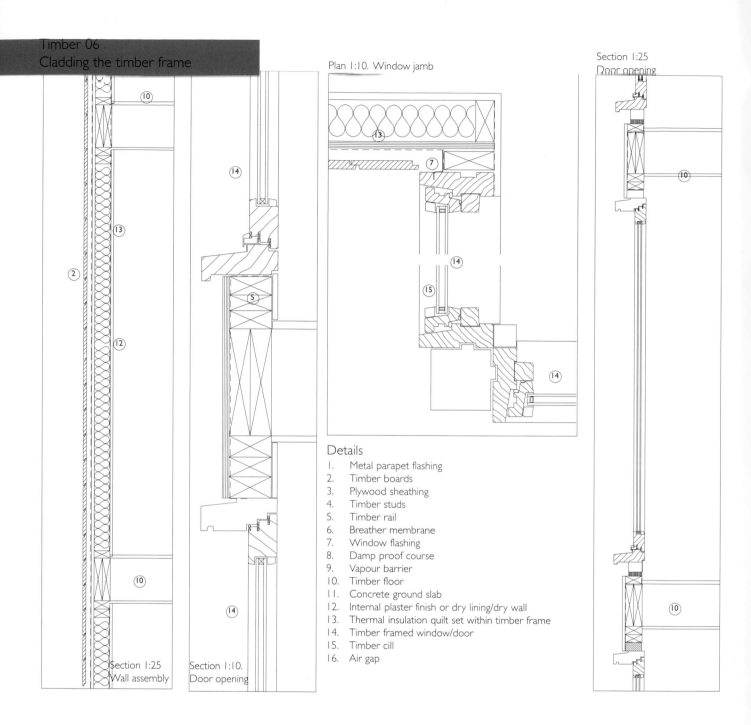

Plan 1:10. Window jamb

Section 1:25
Door opening

Section 1:25
Wall assembly

Section 1:10.
Door opening

Details
1. Metal parapet flashing
2. Timber boards
3. Plywood sheathing
4. Timber studs
5. Timber rail
6. Breather membrane
7. Window flashing
8. Damp proof course
9. Vapour barrier
10. Timber floor
11. Concrete ground slab
12. Internal plaster finish or dry lining/dry wall
13. Thermal insulation quilt set within timber frame
14. Timber framed window/door
15. Timber cill
16. Air gap

Details around windows and doors are as those described in the section on timber window walls in the Glass Chapter.

Timber cladding at ground level stops a minimum of 150mm (6in) above external ground level to avoid rainwater splashing up the timber, which would cause staining and deterioration of the material. Cladding is usually supported at ground level on a concrete slab or edge beam that forms part of the concrete wall. Alternatively, the wall can span between concrete pads at 3000mm-5000mm centres (10ft-16ft), with timber beams at the base of the wall to provide support between pads. Where a concrete slab is used, the edge of the slab has traditionally

been exposed as a base to the wall. With increasing concerns of increased thermal insulation at the ground level of a building, thermal insulation has been introduced on the visible edge of the slab between ground level and the base of timber cladding. The insulation requires an outer protection to the insulation, typically thin concrete slab or brickwork.

The timber wall frame is not fixed directly to the floor slab but instead is usually set on a continuous timber section, which is first fixed to the concrete slab to provide both a level surface to set the timber in place and to be an easier fixing to use than simply nailing. A damp proof course (DPC) is

set beneath the continuous timber base plate to protect the timber, the DPC usually extending down the vertical face of the concrete slab where it connects with the damp proof membrane (DPM) beneath the concrete slab or the vertical face of the basement wall. The DPC will also be continuous with a DPM set on top of the concrete slab. Floor finishes are then applied in the same depth as the continuous baseplate, allowing internal skirting boards to be fixed to the bottom rail of the timber frame, which sits at the finished floor level. Where concrete pads are used, the timber beam is set into stainless steel shoes which are fixed to the concrete pads. The pads may extend below ground level to form foundations where the

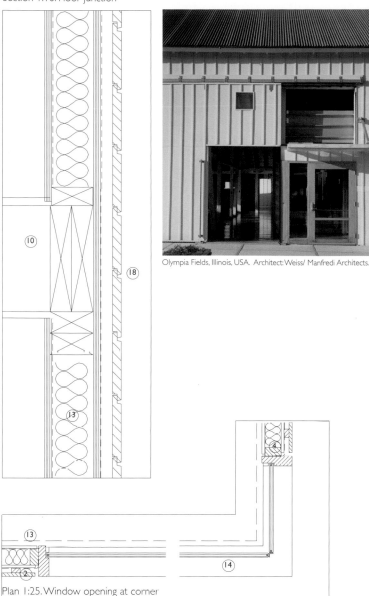

Olympia Fields, Illinois, USA. Architect: Weiss/ Manfredi Architects.

Plan 1:25. Window opening at corner

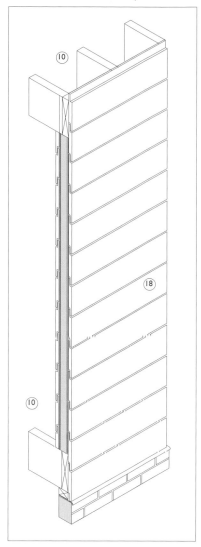

ground is allowed to continue underneath the building. Alternatively, the panels may sit on a concrete floor slab set below the timber ground floor to prevent the growth of any vegetation beneath the raised ground floor. Gravel is often set at ground level in the void below a raised timber floor. Door thresholds at ground level usually have a raised profile to prevent water from penetrating through the opening, and these are also fixed directly onto the continuous baseplate. An additional DPC is set on top of the baseplate to avoid moisture penetration through the door threshold.

Timber can also be supported on brick walls set at a minimum of 150mm (6in)

above external ground level and be supported on a concrete strip foundation or ground beam. As bricks go below ground they usually change to either a dense concrete block or a dense engineering quality brick. A raised floor is then set into this brick wall. The void beneath the timber floor is ventilated with air bricks that encourage cross ventilation. This avoids stagnant air in the void from damaging and eventually rotting the timber floor. Instead of supporting the floor on the brick wall, floors can be supported separately as pads, typically in mild galvanised or stainless steel posts. This allows the ground floor slabs to be built before the timber wall is started, and avoids any risk of long term damage to the floor joists from contact with

a damp wall below DPC level. An alternative method of supporting the low level brickwork is on stainless steel lintels spanning between the concrete pads that support the timber floor. The brick base can be avoided completely by the use of beams spanning between concrete panels as described previously.

Upper floors

Timber framed wall panels are used to support upper floors also in timber. Floor joists are set directly into the timber frame, where they are supported, either on the top of the floor-height panel below, or to the sides of the timber studs if the floor extends over the two or more floors in the balloon

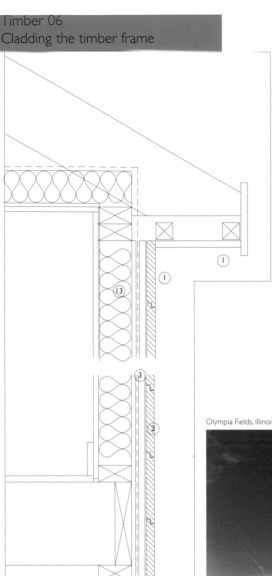

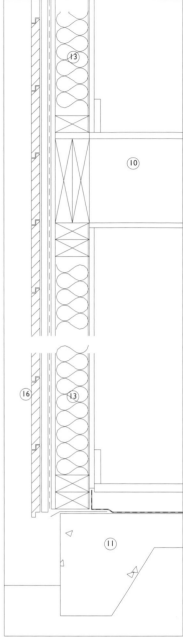

Sections 1-10 Floor junction, eaves to pitched roof,
2 ground conditions

Details
1. Metal parapet flashing
2. Timber boards
3. Plywood sheathing
4. Timber studs
5. Timber rail
6. Breather membrane
7. Window flashing
8. Damp proof course
9. Vapour barrier
10. Timber floor
11. Concrete ground slab
12. Internal plaster finish or dry lining/dry wall
13. Thermal insulation quilt set within timber frame
14. Timber framed window/door
15. Timber cill
16. Air gap

Olympia Fields, Illinois, USA. Architect: Weiss/ Manfredi Architects.

frame. Where timber wall frames span only from floor to floor, as is more commonly the case, floor joists are fixed to the face of timber beams that form part of the wall frame instead of penetrating the frame itself. This allows the gap between wall and floor to be filled with timber, which drastically reduces sound transmission between floors. Because the timber floor and wall form a continuous structure, there is no need to form a horizontal movement in the timber cladding outside. This gives the continuous surface of timber cladding across two or three floors that is characteristic of platform frame construction.

Corners
The most common corner formed in timber cladding is a single timber bead set so that the timber boards on both sides butt into the corner bead. If a breather membrane is used behind the cladding, then an additional waterproof flashing is added to the corner. This is formed in a durable polymer-based sheet or metal sheet. Alternatively, the boards can be allowed to make a corner with a butt joint, and an additional L-shaped timber trim, formed from two separate timber sections, is added on the face of the corner to protect the exposed end grain of one of the sides forming the corner. These trims also provide a visual tidiness to the corners. Boards can be joined with a mitred

joint (45°) without any cover strip but the timber used must be of the highest quality to avoid the joint opening up with moisture movement, and very high levels of workmanship are required. A waterproof layer or flashing behind the mitred joint is essential to the waterproofing performance of this detail. Internal corners are formed using the same sets of timber beads or mitred joints.

Roof eaves and parapets
Overhanging eaves from pitched roofs or flat roofs are very common with timber cladding as they provide protection to the wall beneath from the worst effects of weathering from water running directly down the facade. A continuous timber sec-

Section 1:10. 2 eaves conditions to pitched roofs

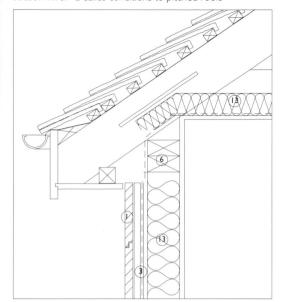

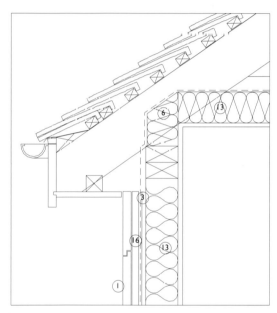

Isometric view of wall assembly

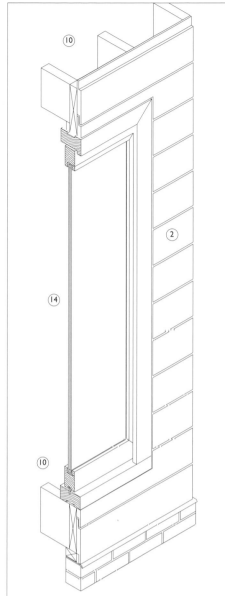

Section 1:25. Wall assembly

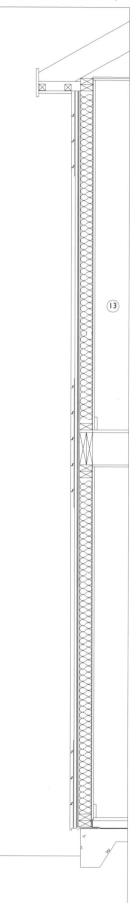

tion, or wallplate, is set on top of the timber frame, creating a double thickness of timber at the top of the wall. This serves as a base for sloping rafters or for flat joists. For large scale roof structures, deeper timber sections are used, set on end, as used for connections to upper floor structures. The waterproof layer on the outside of the timber framing, or breather membrane, is made continuous with that of the roof structure. In the case of overhanging eaves, the roof may be ventilated or be sealed, but in both cases the membranes must be continuous to avoid water penetrating the joint. On the inside face of the wall, the vapour barrier must be continuous from wall to roof, or wall to ceiling level, beneath the roof.

Isometric views of wall assembly

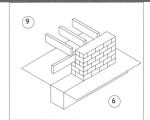

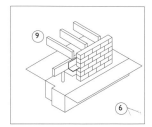

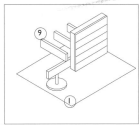

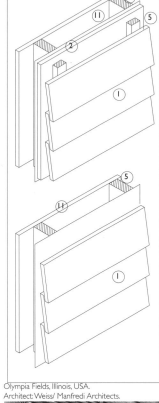

Isometric views of wall assembly at ground level

Details

1. Timber boards
2. Plywood sheathing
3. Timber studs
4. Timber rail
5. Breather membrane
6. Foundation
7. Damp proof course
8. Vapour barrier
9. Timber floor
10. Concrete floor
11. Internal finish
12. Thermal insulation quilt set within timber frame
13. Timber framed window/door
14. Timber cill
15. Air gap

Olympia Fields, Illinois, USA.
Architect: Weiss/ Manfredi Architects.

16. Sliding timber louvre panel
17. Metal facing
18. External plywood facing
19. Cover strip
20. External floor deck
21. External glass wall in twin wall
22. Structural timber frame

Timber boards

Timber boards for cladding panels and rainscreens are sawn and are available in many timber species, though environmental concerns have led to an increasing preference for locally-grown timber for large-scale applications. This is because timber has a negative effect on CO_2 levels, reducing the levels in the atmosphere. The CO_2 emissions created as a result of cutting and working timber before it reaches a local building site is still less than the amount of CO_2 consumed by the timber during its growth. The highest timber grades are used for wall cladding boards, since exposure to the weather will involve considerable temperature and humidity variations, as well as fading in sunlight. Softwoods

are generally used for the cladding of timber frames, with hardwoods being more commonly used for cladding panel and rainscreen applications. Where hardwoods are used, those species that are naturally durable are used. Where less expensive, less durable timbers are used, these require higher levels of finishing and maintenance. For softwoods, preservative treatment is used, but with an increasing scrutiny of the methods, since some preservatives can damage ground around the site as a result of water run-off from the timber into the ground around the timber wall. Softwood boards are made usually in 250mm (10in) widths, with trimmed boards with profiles routed into them usually trimmed down to 150mm - 200mm widths

(6in-8in). Wider boards cannot generally be used due to the risk of the material curving in section.

The increased use of hardwoods in rainscreens, for their durability, has led to different thicknesses and sections of timber being used. This has led to the increased use of louvred timber screens and panels in front of glazed windows and doors to provide solar protection while contributing to the texture of the timber facade.

All timbers vary in moisture content with changes in temperature and air humidity, this being one of the essential aspects to be considered in timber detailing. Most tim-

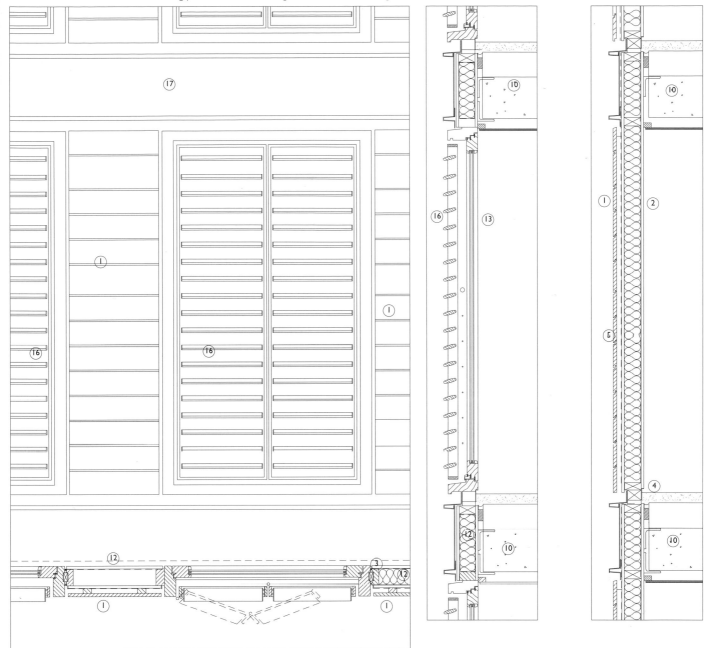

bers used in cladding will have a moisture content from around 5% to 20% when in use. Similar levels are found in timbers from timber suppliers, and are classified as 'dry', 'kiln dried' or 'seasoned'. However, some softwoods are supplied unseasoned, depending on the supplier, so the amount of timber drying and seasoning is critical to the way that timber is cut on site to fit a junction. Unseasoned timber will shrink as it dries, and consequently an allowance is made for later shrinkage by increasing the overlap between timbers where applicable, or making tighter butt joints where these are used. Unseasoned timbers are fixed in place soon after delivery to site to avoid any twisting or warping of the timber. As a result,

lapped boards are not nailed together where they overlap, and nails and screws are secured so that the timber can move without the timber splitting or being damaged.

Finishes

Timber cladding is finished with the timber being left either as supplied, with preservative applied or injected by the supplier, or alternatively is given coats of preservative in clear, stained, or opaque finish on site with preservatives that repel rainwater, or wood stains and paint. Paints can be oil-based or acrylic, while preservatives are clear and can be used as a finish that penetrates the depth of the wood without appreciably changing its appearance. It can also be used before stain-

ing or painting the timber. Preservatives help to prevent moisture absorption as well as reduce fungal growth. This is because they enhance the life of the timber but do not prevent the material changing colour and fading to a silver grey appearance. Site-applied finishes and regular maintenance help overcome the effects of the weathering of timber.

In addition to the use of preservatives and coatings, the orientation of timber boards is critical to the long term performance of timber cladding. The most common types of jointing of boards is 'shiplapping' where timber boards are set horizontally and lapped over one another with the

Section 1:10. Junction with floor slabs

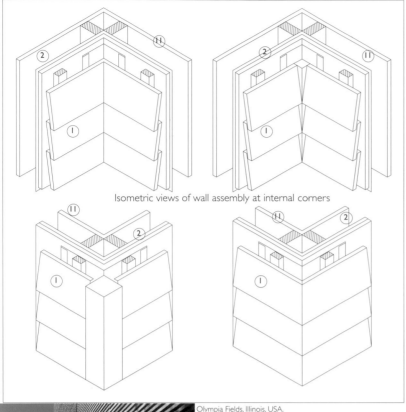

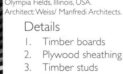

Isometric views of wall assembly at internal corners

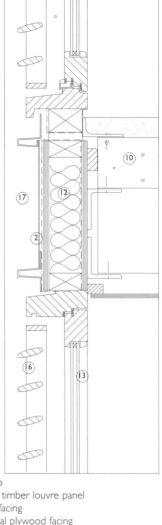

Olympia Fields, Illinois, USA.
Architect: Weiss/ Manfredi Architects.

Details

1. Timber boards
2. Plywood sheathing
3. Timber studs
4. Timber rail
5. Breather membrane
6. Foundation
7. Damp proof course
8. Vapour barrier
9. Timber floor
10. Concrete floor
11. Internal finish
12. Thermal insulation quilt set within timber frame
13. Timber framed window/door
14. Timber cill
15. Air gap
16. Sliding timber louvre panel
17. Metal facing
18. External plywood facing
19. Cover strip
20. External floor deck
21. External glass wall in twin wall
22. Structural timber frame

upper board lapped over the top of the board below to protect it from rainwater ingress. Shiplapping can be assisted by the use of 'feathered' or wedge-shaped boards to give the lapping a more elegant appearance. Tongue-and-groove boards are used to give a continuous flat appearance, while having the advantage of locking boards together into a continuous plate-like structure. Boards are typically around 20mm (0.75in) thick, made as long as possible at around 3000mm - 3500mm (10ft-11ft6in), to avoid vertical joints which are a potential source of rainwater penetration except in rainscreen configuration. Where tongue-and-groove boards are used, the groove is set on the underside to avoid water accumulating when the boards

are set horizontally or diagonally. Where tongue-and-groove boards are set vertically, the groove is set away from the prevailing wind direction to avoid windblown rain being blown into the joint. Joints between boards are never sealed along their long edges with silicone or mastic sealants as this prevents the timber from drying properly, which would cause the material to deteriorate and eventually rot. However, sealants are used on the ends of timber boards when the complete external surface is sealed with paint.

Cladding panels and rainscreens

Timber cladding to a platform frame or a balloon frame is continuous, forming an

integral part of the wall structure. In contrast, timber cladding panels are fixed to building frames in reinforced concrete, steel and timber. In this application, cladding panels follow the principle of other forms of cladding, requiring pre-fabrication of panels and allowance for structural movement in the supporting frame associated with larger-scale structures. Cladding panels can also be faced with plywood rather than timber boards, in rainscreen applications. Because of the higher moisture movement associated with timber than with other materials, junctions between cladding panels require allowance for movement as a result of changing moisture levels in the material.

Elevations: Typical build-up of cladding panel

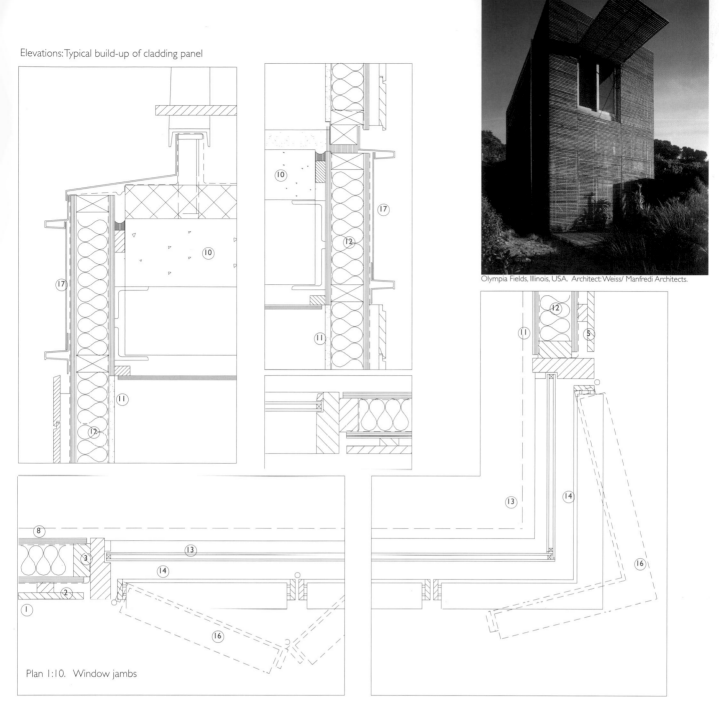

Olympia Fields, Illinois, USA. Architect: Weiss/ Manfredi Architects.

Plan 1:10. Window jambs

When reinforced concrete or steel frames are used, the timber cladding panels are set forward of the floor slabs in the manner of glazed curtain walling. Panels extend from floor to floor, being either hung from a floor slab or else sitting on a bracket on the floor below. In taller buildings, timber cladding is used in conjunction with a twin wall construction with an inner timber wall and an outer open jointed glazed wall. The outer glazed wall provides protection against wind, dust and noise, allowing the windows to be opened for natural ventilation. The outer wall provides a 'thermal buffer' to reduce the effects of heat and cold at different times of the year. The two walls are set 700mm - 1000mm (2ft3in-3ft3in) apart to

allow access from the inner timber wall to the zone between the two walls for maintenance and cleaning access. The outer glass screen also provides protection to the timber cladding from the effects of rain and wind, allowing the material to maintain its appearance without full exposure to outside conditions. Vertical joints between panels have a stepped joint to allow for deflections in floor slabs between panels, following principles of glazed curtain walling. This stepped joint is covered on the outside with timber boards, set forward of the face of panels on battens in rainscreen configuration. The construction of panels follows the same principle of timber cladding described in the previous section. Horizontal joints have an inner

chamber formed between two adjacent panels. Any rainwater that penetrates the outer seal, which is also kept open in some designs, is drained down an inner chamber where the water is discharged through the horizontal joint at floor level. The outer timber cladding has continuous vertical joints to allow panels to be fixed sequentially, unless the outer timber boards are applied after the panels have been installed, but this is contrary to the panel-based form of construction.

Where timber frames are used to support timber cladding panels, cladding is set between floor structures rather than forward of them, since there is no significant thermal bridge from outside to inside, allow-

Section 1:25.

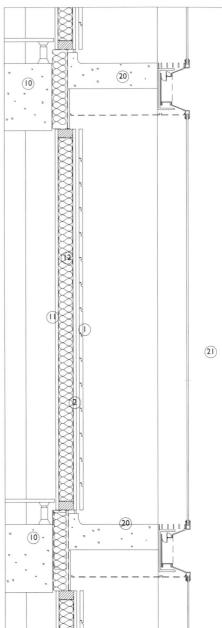

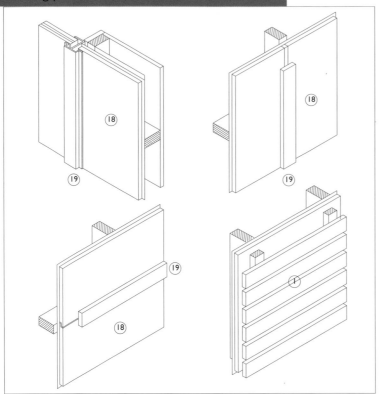

Plan 1:25 Typical cladding panel with additional solar shading or guarding, allowing door to be opened above ground level if panel is fixed closed.

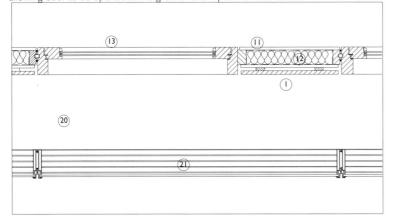

ing the structural frame to be exposed on the outside. Where timber frames are exposed, laminated timber is often used, since it can be formed in beams of significant loadbearing capacity, and is able to form a frame rather than the continuous loadbearing wall of the platform frame. Cladding panels are set into openings in the laminated timber frame, with panels supported at their base on the tops of beams. Floor decks in timber are then fixed to the side of the laminated timber beams. Timber panels are fixed at their base to the beam beneath, but have a sliding restraint at the top to allow the slab and panel above to deflect without damaging the panel below. A metal flashing at the base of the panel drains water at its base and

throws it clear of the beam beneath in order to avoid staining of the timber beam. The outer timber rainscreen cladding is set flush with the outer face of the laminated timber frame to avoid any views into the water-proofing layer behind.

The use of computer numerically controlled (CNC) machines ensures the accurate cutting of components to make timber wall panels with the close tolerances of high quality, large scale construction, particularly housing, where timber has undergone a huge revival, partly due to its lower levels of embodied energy in its construction. The use of composite aluminium / timber windows, with their high performance, low U-values and acoustic attenuation, has given timber

cladding panels greater impetus for large scale projects where traditionally the thermal and weather resisting performance of timber windows and frames has been much poorer than that of aluminium or UPVC windows and doors.

Plywood sheets

When plywood sheets are used with timber cladding panels, the edges of the sheets are protected, since the edges of plywood are susceptible to damage and rot if left exposed in an external environment. Edges can be protected with metal trims and flashings, where an aluminium Z-shaped profile is set on the back of one sheet, projecting out through a vertical or horizontal joint,

Section 1:25.
Cladding panel in twin wall configuration for taller buildings.

Elevation and plan 1:25.
Cladding panel in twin wall configuration for taller buildings.

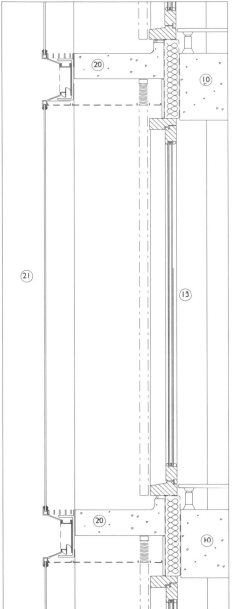

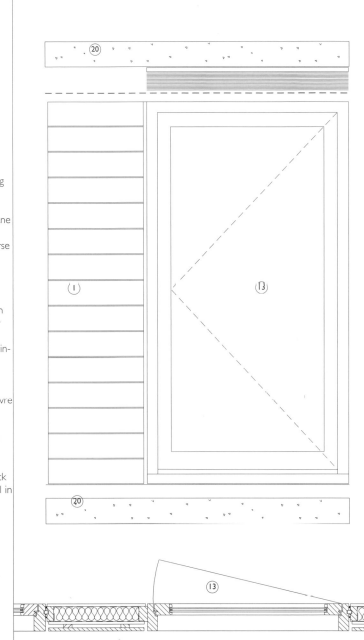

Details
1. Timber boards
2. Plywood sheathing
3. Timber studs
4. Timber rail
5. Breather membrane
6. Foundation
7. Damp proof course
8. Vapour barrier
9. Timber floor
10. Concrete floor
11. Internal finish
12. Thermal insulation quilt set within timber frame
13. Timber framed window/door
14. Timber cill
15. Air gap
16. Sliding timber louvre panel
17. Metal facing
18. External plywood facing
19. Cover strip
20. External floor deck
21. External glass wall in twin wall
22. Structural timber frame

and is set over the face of the adjacent panel. Timber strips can also be set over joints to protect the outside face of the plywood but also allow the rear face to be ventilated into a cavity to allow the material to be kept dry. Since plywood sheets can now be supplied in very large sizes, bays of plywood can be made from a single sheet, reducing the need for edge protection of the plywood. Plywood sheets are also lapped in the horizontal joints to create a visual effect like shiplapped timber boards, or are shingled in the manner of sheet metal cladding. The increased use of rainscreen timber cladding with a waterproof backing wall has increased the freedom for timber panel design.

Olympia Fields, Illinois, USA. Architect: Weiss/ Manfredi Architects.

Cover photo:
Carter/Tucker House, Breamlea,
Victoria, Australia.
Architect: Sean Godsell Architects.
Photo by Earl Carter.

1. Sheet metal
War Museum, Manchester,
England.
Architect: Daniel Libeskind
Photos by Christian Richters.

2. Profiled cladding
Mini-House, Nerima-ku, Tokyo,
Japan.
Architect: Tsukamoto and Kaijima /
Atelier Bow-Wow, TIT Tsukamoto
Lab. Photos courtesy of Yoshiharu
Tsukamoto.

3. Composite panels
Telecom Authority Building,
Oporto, Portugal.
Architect: João Álvaro Rocha and
José Manuel Gigante.
Photos by Luís Ferreira Alves.

4. Rainscreens
Bridgewatchers House,
Rotterdam, Holland.
Architect: Bolles + Wilson.
Photos by Christian Richters.

5. Mesh screens
Kew House, Melbourne, Australia.
Architect: Sean Godsell Architects.
Photos by -Earl Carter.

6. Louvre screens
British School in the Netherlands,
The Hague, Holland.
Architect: Kraaijvanger Urbis.
Photos by Jan Derwig and P. de
Ruig.

7. Stick systems
University Library, Delft, Holland.
Architect: Mecanoo architekten bv.
Photos by Christian Richters.

8. Panel systems
RWE AG Essen, Germany.
Architect: Ingenhoven Overdiek
Photos by H. G. Esch, Holger
Knauf.

9. Clamped glazing
Mediatheque, Sendai, Japan.

Architect: Toyo Ito & Associates.
Photos by Dana Buntrock.

10. Bolt fixed glazing
Hong Kong Station.
Architect: Arup Associates.
Photos by Christian Richters.

11a. Cast glass channels
Town Hall and Theatre, Ijsselstein,
Holland.
Architect: UN studio van Berkel &
Bos. Photos by Christian Richters.

11b. Glass blocks
Hermes Building, Tokyo.
Architect: Renzo Piano Building
Workshop.
Photos by M. Denancé, courtesy
of Renzo Piano Building
Workshop.

12. Steel windows
Spanish-Portuguese Cultural
Centre, Zamora, Spain.
Architect: Manuel de las Casas.
Photos by Angel Baltanas.

13. Aluminium and PVC-U win-
dows
Patio Houses, Esposende, Portugal.
Architect: João Álvaro Rocha.
Photos by Luís Ferreira Alves.

14. Timber windows
Housing, Tilburg, Holland.
Architect: (EEA) Erick van Egeraat
associated architects.
Photos by Christian Richters.

15. Cast in situ / Cast-in-place
CAC Museum, Cincinnati, USA.
Architect: Zaha Hadid Architects.
Photos by Roland Halbe.

16. Storey height precast panels
Parking Building, Takasaki, Japan.
Architect: Kengo Kuma &
Associates.
Photos courtesy of Kengo Kuma.

17. Small precast cladding panels
Palacio de Congresos, Santiago de
Compostela, Spain.
Architect: Alberto Noguerol y
Pilar Diez Architects.
Photos by Leopoldo A. Lamberti,
courtesy of Tectónica magazine.

18. Masonry loadbearing walls
Rehabilitation Center for
Handicapped Children, Perbál,
Hungary.
Architect: Janesch / Karacsony
Photos courtesy of Janesch /
Karacsony.

19. Masonry cavity walls: Brick
Moderna Museet, Stockholm.
Architect: Rafael Moneo
Arquitectos.
Photos by Roland Halbe.

20. Masonry cavity walls: Stone
and concrete block
Town Hall, Valdemqueda, Spain.
Architect: García de
Paredes/Pedrosa. Photos courtesy
of Paredes/Pedrosa.

21. Masonry cladding
City Hall, Murcia, Spain.
Architect: Rafael Moneo Arq.
Photos by Roland Halbe.

22. Masonry rainscreens
Potsdamer Platz, Berlin.
Architect: Renzo Piano Building
Workshop.
Photos by M. Denancé, E. Como,
Vincent Mosch, and Berengo
Gardin, courtesy of Renzo Piano
Building Workshop.

23. Plastic sealed panels
Cinema, Rotterdam, Holland.
Architect: Koen van Velsen.
Photos by Kim Zwarts.

24. Plastic Rainscreens
House, Kawagoe, Japan.
Architect: Shigeru Ban Architects.
Photos by Hiroyuki Hirai.

25. Cladding the timber frame
Olympia Fields, Illinois, USA.
Architect: Weiss/ Manfredi
Photos by Bruce Van Inwegen,
Paul Warchol and Tim Hursley
courtesy of Weiss/ Manfredi.

26. Cladding panels and rain-
screens
Carter/Tucker House, Breamlea,
Victoria, Australia.
Architect: Sean Godsell Architects.
Photos by Earl Carter.

Andrew Watts conceived the book, wrote the text, drew the illustrations on CAD and set out the pages. Andrew Watts has 20 years' experience working as an architect specialising in facade detailing on international projects with a wide range of construction technologies. He was a project architect for Jean Nouvel in Paris, working on some of his most notable buildings. Andrew Watts has a Masters Degree from the University of Cambridge in Interdisciplinary Design. More recently as a facade specialist, he has worked on some well-known projects around the world including Federation Square, Melbourne, and the Millennium Bridge, London. He presented a paper on passive and low energy design to the PLEA Conference 2000. Andrew Watts is currently a facade specialist on the Bur Juman Project in Dubai, one of the largest facade projects in the Middle East. He is working on a companion volume in the Modern Construction series. Andrew can be contacted at awatts@newtec-nic.com.

Yasmin Watts designed the book. She undertook both the illustrations and the graphic design of the layouts. Yasmin Watts was an architect at the Renzo Piano Building Workshop in Paris, where she worked on the Cultural Centre in New Caledonia, and the Cité Internationale in Lyon, France. Yasmin can be contacted at: ywatts@newtecnic.com.

The German language edition of this book has been translated by Norma Kessler, who has adapted the book for use in the German-speaking countries.

David Marold is Editor for Architecture and Building Techniques at Springer Verlag in Vienna. He has driven this book from a set of basic layouts to a completed book. He has a passion for books and their design, ranging from their wider content to the quality of print paper.

AUTHOR'S THANKS

I would like to thank my mother, Mrs Helena Watts, for proof reading in the final stages. I would also like to thank the following people for providing photographic images: Grant Suzuki of Shigeru Ban Architects, Jan Rinke of Architekturbüro Bolles Wilson, Manuel de las Casas, Catrin Schal of (EEA) Erick van Egeraat associated architects, Hayley Franklin of Sean Godsell Architects, Zaha Hadid Architects, Ute Einhoff of Ingenhoven, Overdiek und Partner, Mariko Nishimura of Toyo Ito & Associates, Peter Janesch and Tamas Karacsony, Karin Wolf of Kraaijvanger-Urbis Architects, Hidemi Baba of Kengo Kuma & Associates, Daniel Libeskind Architects, Machteld Schoep of Mecanoo Architekten, Sandra Rush of Rafael Moneo Arquitectos, Ove Arup and Partners, Alberto Noguerol and Pilar Diez, Angela García de Paredes of Paredes / Pedrosa Arquitectos, Chiara Casazza at Renzo Piano Building Workshop, Antonio Neves of João Álvaro Rocha Arquitectos, Yoshiharu Tsukamoto, UN studio van Berkel & Bos, Koen van Velsen Architects, Patrick Armacost at Weiss Manfredi Architects.

I would like to thank all the following photographers for providing images of their work: Luís Ferreira Alves, Angel Baltanas, Dana Buntrock, Earl Carter, E. Como, M. Denancé, Jan Derwig, H. G. Esch, Berengo Gardin, Roland Halbe, Hiroyuki Hirai, Tim Hursley, Bruce Van Inwegen, Holger Knauf, Leopoldo A. Lamberti, Vincent Mosch, Christian Richters, P. de Ruig, Paul Warchol, Kim Zwarts.

ADDITIONAL PHOTOGRAPHS USED IN THE INTRODUCTION

1. Bard Theatre, Annandale NY, USA.
Architect: Frank O Gehry.
Photos by Roland Halbe.

2. Science Park, Valencia, Spain.
Architect: Santiago Calatrava.
Photos by Roland Halbe.

3. Town Hall and Theatre, Ijsselstein, Holland.
Architect: UN studio van Berkel & Bos. Photos by Christian Richters.

4. Hermes Building, Tokyo.
Architect: Renzo Piano Building Workshop.
Photos by M. Denancé, courtesy of Renzo Piano Building Workshop.

5. Peninsula House.
Victoria, Australia.
Architect: Sean Godsell Architects.
Photos by Earl Tucker.

6. Bridgewatchers House, Rotterdam, Holland.
Architect: Bolles + Wilson.
Photos by Christian Richters.

All other photographs in introduction essays are by the author.

This bibliography lists articles from the international technical press from the years 1990 to 2003. The subject matter of these articles covers general issues about the nature and the future of facade construction, from a materials-based standpoint.

AA FILES
no. 31, Summer 1996.
'Truth to material' vs 'the principle of cladding': the language of materials in architecture.

A+T
no. 14, 1999.
Special issue. Materiales sensibles [Sensitive materials].

ARCA
no. 129, September 1998.
Special issue. Superfici [Surfaces].

ARCHITECT (THE HAGUE)
vol. 30, no. 5, May 1999.
Grotere rijkheid met eenvoudiger middelen. Vlies- en metselwekgevels van Rudy Uytenhaak [Greater richness with a choice of materials. Prefabrication and preshaping of materials are the primary methods used].

ARQUITECTURA VIVA
no. 54, May/June 1997.
Berlin de piedra. Revestimientos de fachada: ?variedad en la unidad? [Berlin in stone. Recladding facades: variety in unity?]

ARCHITECTURE NEW ZEALAND
May/June, 1999.
Skin game.

ARCHITECTURE INTERIEURE CREE
no. 289, 1999.
Special issue. Friches / renovation / reconversion [Renovation and conversion of disused buildings].

ARCHITECTURE MOUVEMENT CONTINUITE
no. 20, April 1988.
Facades industrielles [Industrial facades].

ARCHITECTURE TODAY
no. 98, May 1999.
Innovation: a vision of the construction industry twenty years from now predicts far-reaching changes.

ARCHITECTURAL RECORD

October 1995.
The Intelligent Exterior.

ARCHITECTURAL REVIEW
vol. 194, no. 1167, May 1994.
Special issue. Materiality.

ARCHITECTURAL REVIEW
January 1995.
Light spirited.

ARCHITECTURAL REVIEW
vol. 202, no. 1208, October 1997.
Special issue. Nature of materials.

ARCHITECTURAL REVIEW
vol. 207, no. 1239, May 2000.
Special issue. Materiality.

ARCHITECTURAL REVIEW
May 2002.
Material witnesses.

ARCHITECTURAL REVIEW
February 2003.
The New Paradigm in Architecture.

ARCHITECTURAL REVIEW
June 2003.
The search for climate responsive architecture.

ARCHITEKT
no. 1, January 1997.
Okologische Bewertung von Baustoffen [The ecological assessment of construction materials].

ARCHITEKT
no. 5, May 1998.
Special issue. Fassade - Gesicht, Haut oder Hulle? [A facade - the face, the skin or the cladding?]

ARCHITEKT
no. 11, November 1999.
Special issue. Im Reich der Erfindung [In the realm of invention].

ARCHITEKT
no. 3, March 2000.
Planung und Ausfuhrung: Glasfassaden [Design and implementation: glass facades].

ARCHITEKTUR (BERLIN)
vol. 40, no. 8, August 1991.
Vorgehangte Fassaden [Facades].

ARCHITHESE
vol. 22, no. 3, May/June 1992.
Special issue. Nur Fassade [Facades].

BAUMEISTER
vol. 93, no. 8, August 1996.
Neue Baustoffe [New materials].

BAUMEISTER
vol. 95, no. 7, July 1998.
Special issue. Neue Oberflachen - Material als architektonisches Programm [New surfaces - materials as architectural programme].

BAUWELT
vol. 87, no. 16, April 26, 1996.
Aufs Ganze gehen Glasfassaden [Go all the way with glass facades].

BAUWELT
vol. 87, no. 43/44, November 22, 1996.
Auf dem Prufstand [From the test bed].

BAUWELT
vol. 88, no. 7, February 1997.
Naturstein [Natural stone].

BAUWELT
vol. 91, no. 3, January 21, 2000
Von den Materialien [On materials].

CASABELLA
June 1996
Le pareti ventilate [Ventilated walls].

DETAIL
vol. 30, no. 4, August/September 1990.
Special issue. Fassaden-Konstruktionen [Facade systems].

DETAIL
vol. 33, no. 3, June/July 1993.
Special issue. Metallfassaden [Metal facade constructions].

DETAIL
vol. 36, no. 4, June 1996.
Special issue. Fassade, Fenster [Facades and fenestration].

DETAIL
vol. 38, no. 1, January/February 1998.
Special issue. Einfaches Bauen [Simple forms of building].

DETAIL
vol. 38, no. 7, October/November 1998.
Special issue. Fassaden [Facades].

DETAIL
July 2001
Facades

DETAIL
July/August 2003.
Facades/Envelopes.

DEUTSCHE BAUZEITSCHRIFT
vol. 38, no. 4, April 1990.
Fassaden mit Stahlbauteilen [Facades with
steel elements].

DEUTSCHE BAUZEITSCHRIFT
vol. 40, no. 8, August 1992.
Die Dreidimensionalitat der Fassaden-
Verschraubung [The three dimensionality
of screwing together facades].

DEUTSCHE BAUZEITSCHRIFT
vol. 45, no. 5, May 1997.
Auswahl von Baumaterialien. Gegenwartige
trends und zukunftiges Potential [Choice of
building materials. Contemporary trends
and future potential].

DEUTSCHE BAUZEITUNG
vol. 130, no. 1, January 1996.
Materialien [Materials].

DEUTSCHE BAUZEITUNG
vol. 131, no. 10, October 1997.
Chemie im Schafspelz? Dammstoffe aus
Altpapier oder Naturfasern - (k)eine
Alternative? [Insulating material from old
paper or natural fibre - an alternative/no
alternative?]

DEUTSCHE BAUZEITUNG
vol. 133, no. 8, August 1999.
Fluch und Segen [PVC recycling in building
materials].

DOMUS
no. 756, January 1994.
Materiali e progetto [Materials and design].

DOMUS
no. 789, January 1997.
Leapfrog - progettare la sostenibilita
[Leapfrog - designing sustainability].

DOMUS
no. 801, February 1998.
Materialita [Materiality].

DOMUS
no. 818, September 1999.

Special issue. Impara dalla natura [Learning
from nature].

ECO
vol. 38, no. 7, October/November 1998.
For green, try blue.

ECO DESIGN
vol. 6, no. 2, 1998.
Special issue. Eco design around the world.

GLASFORUM
vol. 39, no. 3, June 1989.
Tendenzen der Glasarchitektur:
Glasfassadenkonzepte aus England [Trends
in glass architecture: glass facades from
England].

MONITEUR ARCHITECTURE AMC
no. 22, June 1991.
Details: les facades metalliques [Details:
metal facades].

MONITEUR ARCHITECTURE AMC
no. 70, April 1996.
Facades: les bardages metalliques [Facades:
metal cladding].

MONITEUR ARCHITECTURE AMC
no. 75, November 1996.
Facade: panneaux de bois [Facades: timber
panels].

MONITEUR ARCHITECTURE AMC
no. 83, October 1997.
Les facades.

PROGRESSIVE ARCHITECTURE,
February 1994.
What makes a good curtain wall?

PROGRESSIVE ARCHITECTURE
March 1994.
The ends of finishing.

PROGRESSIVE ARCHITECTURE
June 1994.
Amazing glazing.

QUADERNS
No.202, 1994.
La flexibilidad come dispositivo [Flexibility
as a device].

RECUPERARE
vol. 10, no. 9, November/December 1991.
La valutazione delle facciate ventilate [The
evaluation of ventilated facades].

RECUPERARE EDILIZIA DESIGN
IMPIANTI
vol. 2, no. 8, November/December 1983.
Ventilated facades in building rehabilitation.

SOLAR ENERGY
June 1996.
Numerical study of a ventilated facade
panel.

TECHNIQUES & ARCHITECTURE
December-January 1994.
Facade Legere et menuiserie metallique
[Lightweight facades and metal joinery].

TECHNIQUES & ARCHITECTURE
no. 413, April/May 1994.
La dimension ecologique [The ecological
dimension].

TECHNIQUES & ARCHITECTURE
no. 422, October/November 1995.
Revetements de facade [Covering facades].

TECHNIQUES & ARCHITECTURE
no. 430, February/March 1997.
Beton en parement [Concrete as adorn-
ment].

TECHNIQUES & ARCHITECTURE
no. 448, April/May 2000.
De la matiere [Material matters].

TECHNIQUES & ARCHITECTURE
October 2002.
Matériaux innovants et applications à
l'usage des architectes.
(Innovative materials and applications for
the use of architects).

TECHNIQUES & ARCHITECTURE
June-July 2003.
Matériaux imprimés, gravés, sculptés, séri-
graphiés en façade
(Printed, etched, sculpted, serigraphed
façade materials).

WORLD ARCHITECTURE
no. 33, 1995.
Smart cars versus smart facades.

WORLD ARCHITECTURE
no. 47, June 1996.
The art of glass.

WORLD ARCHITECTURE
no. 48, July/August 1996.
Cladding and roofing.

INDEX

Andrew Watts
London, England

© 2005 Springer-Verlag/Wien
Printed in Austria
Springer-VerlagWienNewYork is a part of Springer Science+Business Media
springeronline.com

Printing: Holzhausen Druck & Medien GmbH, A-1140 Wien

Printed on acid-free and chlorine-free bleached paper – TCF
SPIN: 10916926

With numerous (partly coloured) Figures

ISBN 3-211-00638-9 Springer-Verlag WienNew York